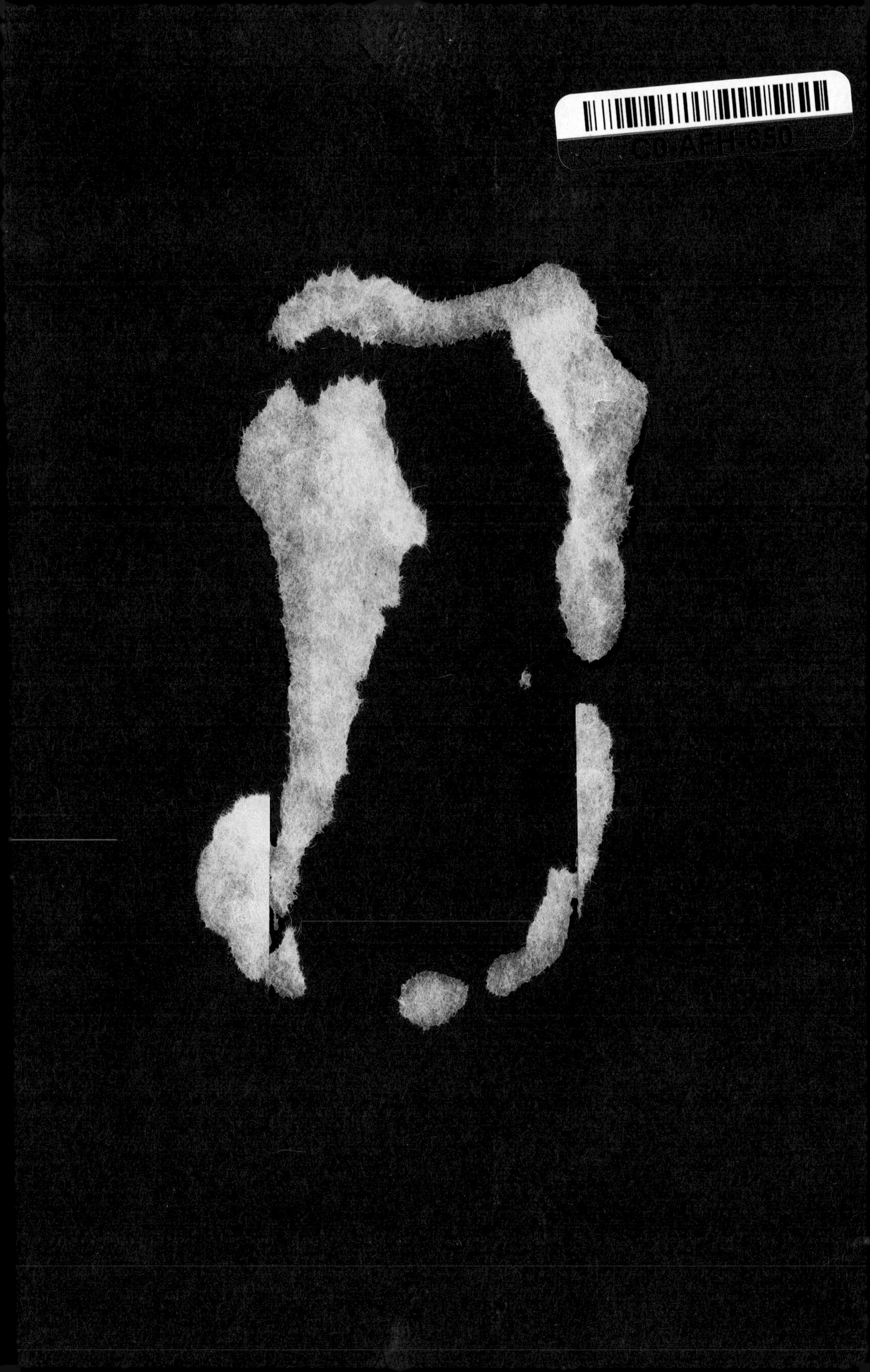
CO AFH 650

INVASION 1066

INVASION 1066

By Rupert Furneaux

PRENTICE-HALL, INC.

Englewood Cliffs, N. J.

Second printing........ May, 1967

Invasion: 1066
by Rupert Furneaux

Library of Congress Catalog Card Number: 66–15193

Printed in the United States of America

T 50219

Prentice-Hall International, Inc., *London*
Prentice-Hall of Australia, Pty., Ltd., *Sydney*
Prentice-Hall of Canada, Ltd., *Toronto*
Prentice-Hall of India (Private) Ltd., *New Delhi*
Prentice-Hall of Japan, Inc., *Tokyo*

Books by Rupert Furneaux

THE FIRST WAR CORRESPONDENT

THE OTHER SIDE OF THE STORY

FACT, FAKE OR FABLE?

THE MAN BEHIND THE MASK

MYTH AND MYSTERY

FAMOUS CRIMINAL CASES I–VII

THE MEDICAL MURDERER

THE SIEGE OF PLEVNA

(IN U.S.A., THE BREAKFAST WAR)

TRIED BY THEIR PEERS

LEGEND AND REALITY

TOBIAS FURNEAUX, CIRCUMNAVIGATOR

THE TWO STRANGERS OF RILLINGTON PLACE

THE WORLD'S STRANGEST MYSTERIES

CRIME DOCUMENTARY:

1. *Guenther Podola*
2. *Robert Hoolhouse*
3. *The Murder of Lord Erroll*
4. *Michael Davies*

COURT ROOM U.S.A., I AND II

THE ZULU WAR (GREAT BATTLES OF HISTORY)

THE MYSTERY OF THE EMPTY TOMB

MASSACRE AT AMRITSAR

WHAT HAPPENED ON THE MARY CELESTE

GREAT ISSUES IN PRIVATE COURTS

NEWS OF WAR

KRAKATOA

Acknowledgments

I am most grateful to the following for their help and assistance:

The Astronomer Royal (for times of sunrise and sunset and information respecting Halley's Comet); the Hydrographic Department of the Admiralty (times of high tides in September 1066); Mr. Trevor Baker (Meteorologist, Southern Television, for "weather forecasts" based on knowledge of the weather in the summer of 1066); Britains Ltd. and Mr. John Gerald Carter (for the loan of toy soldiers and for photographing my "representation" of the Battle of Hastings); Meridian Air Maps Ltd. (for taking an aerial photograph of the battlefield from my suggested point of view); Jill Swain (for drawing the plan of the Battle of Hastings to my specifications); Diana Heaney (for drawing the map, Invasions, 1066); Lieutenant-Colonel C. H. Lemmon, D.S.O., and Mr. C. T. Chevallier (for their advice on problems of the battlefield); Mr. Albert Wood (the guide at Battle Abbey); Monsieur J. B. Debon (photographer of Saint Lô, Manche, France, who accompanied my daughter and me to the village of Fourneaux-sur-Vire); Monsieur Le Mazurier (the Mayor of that village); Monsieur Philippe Maheut (a resident of Fourneaux-le-Val, near Falaise); Mme. A. Bouvier (of Coutances); Mr. J. Mainwaring Baines (Curator, Hastings Museum); and the Librarian and Sub-librarian of the Hampshire County Library.

On my visit to Normandy in July 1964, I inspected the Bayeux

Tapestry, visited the battlefields of Val-ès-Dunes, Mortemer and Varaville, the estuaries of the Divé and Somme and many places connected with William, Falaise, Rouen, and so forth. I found two villages still named Fourneaux, Fourneaux-le-Val, near Falaise, and Fourneaux-sur-Vire, near Saint Lô. In England, I walked over the battlefield of Hastings five times.

It is advisable to emphasize that my "model" of the battlefield, of which photographs are reproduced, is a "representation" only, designed to overcome the difficulty of visualizing the scene which is now so largely obscured. To have made the model in scale with the toy soldiers would have required sixty feet in length.

RUPERT FURNEAUX

Contents

INVASION 1066

One

The Bequest

The sonorous Latin of the ancient hymn echoes through the Minster. From the door advances a stately procession, bishops, abbots, prelates, earls and thegns. At its head walks the King-elect, led by two bishops, their croziers held aloft. He is bareheaded; his fair hair hangs to his shoulders. Tall and robust of frame, he slows his stride to keep pace with the ambling bishops. The choir sings, praying that the hand of the King-to-be may be strengthened and exalted, that justice and judgment shall be his and that mercy and truth shall go before his face. The long nave and both transepts are crowded. The magnates of England are gathered to acclaim their king. They press back to allow the procession to reach the high altar, before which the King-elect prostrates himself.

The choir chants the Song of Ambrose, as the new ruler rises and turns to face the assembled leaders of the nation, the men who had named him their king the day before. Now he is come to seek God's consecration by sacramental unction, without which he is not fully king.

The choir's chant sinks to a whisper, lost in the roof of the great building. The Archbishop lifts his voice. In ancient form he demands of the assembly whether they will that Harold Godwineson be crowned their lord and king?

The great shout of acclamation rings through the Minster. "Yay, yay, so be it. King Harold. King Harold," assent the great men of the land.

The shout penetrates the walls and is heard outside. The men of England are acclaiming their king, the onlookers know, as they have done at coronations for centuries.

Harold in a loud voice swears the ancient three-fold oath: to preserve peace to the Church of God and to all Christian people, to forbid wrong and robbery to men of every rank within his realm, to enforce justice and mercy, as he would that God would have mercy upon him. And the people cry "Amen."

A bishop prays that the spirit of wisdom may guide the King, for peace to his church and people, and for his welfare in this world and in the next.

Again the Archbishop lifts his voice: In ancient form he prays that God, who wrought his mighty works by the hands of Abraham and Moses, Joshua, David and Solomon, shall shower the gifts and graces he gave them upon he who is now chosen to be the King of the Angles and Saxons. He prays that the new King shall prove as faithful as Abraham, as gentle as Moses, as brave as Joshua, as humble as David and as wise as Solomon, and that he shall rule and guard his church and realm against all visible and invisible foes. He prays that the chosen King may never fail the throne and scepter, and that for the long years of his life he may reign over a faithful people, in peace, concord and, if need be, in victory. And he prays to Christ Himself to raise Harold to the throne of his kingdom and to pour upon him the unction of the Holy One.

The holy act, the sacramental rite, which changes Harold from Earl of Wessex into King of England, follows. The choir sings the anthem that tells how Zadok the Priest and Nathan the Prophet anointed Solomon King of Israel. A bishop prays that, as kings of old were anointed with oil, so may the oil now be poured upon the head of God's servant as a true sign of the inner unction of the heart and a means of His glory and the welfare of His people.

Two bishops lead Harold to his throne. The Archbishop pours the oil upon his head. A succession of prelates vest him in the robes of royalty and give him the insignia of his kingly office. One hands him the Sword with the prayer that he may therewith defend his kingdom and smite his enemies and the enemies of God. Another hands him the Orb of Empire and another the Scepter crowned with a Dove, the symbol of the peaceful days that had followed the expulsion of the Danes.

The Archbishop places the Imperial Diadem of Britain upon Harold's head, imploring God to crown His anointed with glory and justice and to give him a yet brighter crown in a more enduring kingdom. He invokes the blessings of God, of the Virgin Mother of God, of the saints and the Prince of the Apostles upon England's crowned and anointed King.

The assembled people stand and gaze upon their King, anointed and crowned, the Rex Anglorum vel Saxonum *of ancient form.*

King Harold sits upon his royal throne, cloaked in the Imperial Mantle, crown on head, the Orb and the Scepter in his hands. The oaths have been sworn, the holy oil anointed, the prayers prayed. He is truly King of England, named by the magnates of the realm, consecrated before God, crowned and seated upon his throne.

It is a momentous date in English history, 6 January, 1066.

The situation is menacing. Harold and the notables gathered in the New Minster, soon to be named Westminster, know that before long the new king will have to do battle for his crown.

The situation is strange. For the first time in their long history the English people have elected as their king a man who is not of royal blood, who is not even related to the ancient dynasty. By law and custom they have the right to choose whom they will, for the crown of the Anglo-Saxons is both hereditary and elective, vague terms of fluctuating meaning. Necessity rules the choice.

Harold may have tricked or coerced the royal council, the Witan, into electing him king. His coronation in unseemly haste, within a few hours of the old king's death, smacks of a coup d'Etat. Only he, thinks Harold, is capable of steering the nation through the perils to come. Covetous eyes are turned on the fair land of England, seemingly so snug and secure behind its ramparts of turbulent sea. Dark clouds are gathering on the horizon. Two powerful foreign rulers believe that they are the legitimate heirs to the throne. One or both may invade to secure the kingdom they believe theirs by right. To appreciate the situation we need to step back briefly into history.

In the ninth century of our era the Vikings of Scandinavia, the fabled Norsemen, swept down from the north upon Britain and northern France. Within a century they had conquered England, and they also established themselves in France where their domain became known as Normandy.

The Viking empire broke up on the death of King Canute in 1035 and, after his two sons had died, the ancient Anglo-Saxon dynasty, the House of Cerdic, was restored in the person of Edward who, due to his saintliness, became called the Confessor. His mother, Emma, the sister of Duke Richard II of Normandy, had been driven home in exile and Edward had been brought up as a Norman, speaking French. In England, he surrounded himself with Norman friends. His cousin, another Edward, had been forced to take refuge in Hungary. He is known to us as "the Aetheling," a term denoting the first prince of the royal blood.

Edward the Confessor ruled England from 1042 to 1066. During his latter years it became increasingly evident that he would die childless, thus leaving the succession in jeopardy. He had married Edith, the daughter of Earl Godwine, a man who had also sired six sons, the second of whom, Harold, succeeded on his father's death in 1053 to the earldom of Wessex. Harold became England's most powerful subject; nonetheless he needed to tread warily for he controlled only the southern half of the kingdom.

Edward the Confessor had one great ambition, to bequeath his kingdom to his cousin, Duke William of Normandy, and he promised William that he would become King of England upon his death. This bequest was of doubtful validity for promise of the throne by a reigning King, though hallowed by custom, had no authority unless it was ratified by the Witan.

Harold feared the succession of the Norman Duke for there could be no room in William's kingdom for an overpowerful subject. He plotted to secure the succession of a King who would be more amenable to his will; there was an obvious candidate, the Aetheling Edward. He was invited to England in 1057 but he died before he could see the King. He left a son, Edgar, a mere child, who may have been brought to England. He now became the Aetheling. Harold's hopes of securing the succession of a pliant ruler were dashed. The elder Aetheling's death increased the danger of William gaining the throne by virtue of the King's promise, and of Harald Hardrada, the King of Norway, advancing his own claim.

Harald Hardrada believed he was the rightful King by virtue of the pact made by his predecessor, King Magnus of Norway, with Canute's son, Hartha Canute, by which the survivor would inherit the kingdoms of the other. There would be no place in England for a "Sub-regulus," or under-King as Harold was called, under Hardrada, the tyrant of Norway.

Earl Harold schemed to make himself King on Edward's death. He hoped to overcome the fatal objection of lack of royal blood by persuading the old King to nominate him as his successor as a patriotic act. Nevertheless, Harold may have doubted his ability to secure the succession. His alleged oath to support Duke William's candidature, which is discussed in the next chapter, suggests that he was of two minds. If Harold swore such an oath, it lay lightly upon him.

The year 1065 was pregnant with fate. The childless King was reaching the end of his days. News of his declining health was carried to Duke William and to Harald Hardrada. In England, Harold's position was weakened by a bitter quarrel with his brother Tostig, who had been made Earl of Northumbria by the King. When his subjects rose against him, Tostig fled to Flanders, charging Harold with stirring up the revolt in order to get rid of him as a possible rival to the throne. Whatever was the truth of this allegation, the departure of Tostig weakened Harold's position. The King gave the vacant Earldom to Morcar, the younger brother of Earl Edwin of Mercia, both implacable enemies of the ambitious Earl of Wessex.

This eruption of violence and the loss of his friend Tostig plunged King Edward into an illness from which he did not recover. His life's work, the building of the new Minster on the island of Thorney outside the western gate of London, was nearly finished. The last stones were laid in December, but the King was too ill to attend the Minster's consecration on December 28. He was represented by his wife, Edith, and the ceremony was attended by the Witan, assembled in mid-winter session.

It is a time of great anxiety. The old King's days on earth are clearly numbered. When he dies the throne will be vacant. There is no obvious successor; there has not been such doubt for centuries. The next-of-kin, the King's nephew, the old Aetheling's son, Edgar, is still a child, too young to be considered in such dangerous times. The Witan anxiously awaits the King's last words. Cloaked with authority and sanctity his nomination will carry great weight. The story of Edward's promise to William and the rumor of Harold's oath deepen the uncertainty. Neither king nor subject can bequeath or swear away the crown as if it were a piece of land. The decision is the Witan's and its alone.

The chief actors in the drama are assembled in the royal house at Westminster, situated on the spot where the Houses of Parliament now stand. A little group of favored friends gather at the bedside of the dying king. Queen Edith brings the news that the new Minster has been hallowed. The great building is finished. Edward's life work is done. His head sinks back on the pillow. For five days his sickness increases. On the sixth, his speech begins to fail; his voice is feeble, his words incoherent. Then on Thursday, 5 January, his flagging powers rally. He awakens in full possession of his senses. Four people surround his bed. At its head stands the Staller Robert, at its foot sits the Lady Edith, caressing her husband's feet, cold in death. On either side, facing each other across the bed, are the two men who stand to gain or lose most by the King's death. They know the issues at stake. In an hour, a few minutes perhaps, the King will die and the throne will be vacant. The King's bequest, if it is spoken, will have great influence.

Harold and his chief supporter, Archbishop Stigand, know the difficulty of persuading the Witan to elect a king who is not of royal blood, flouting all precedent. Apart from this one defect, Harold fulfills the required conditions. He is experienced in government, an able general, the only man capable of uniting all England against the foes who will surely come. The Witan, he and Stigand believe, needs only the dying King's nomination to choose Harold as England's champion. Its final decision hangs on Edward's words. Harold hopes and prays that the King will speak and speak for him. If he does not, or keeps his promise to William, Harold and Stigand are capable of twisting his words, or inventing the bequest they desire.

Edward's lips part in whispered speech. The listeners crane forward to catch the words. Barely audible comes the sound of a Latin prayer. The whisper dies away, changing to English. The king struggles up. Staller Robert supports him in his arms. He has seen a vision in his slumbers, says Edward. He prayed that he might have strength to declare it. If it were but the phantom of a disordered brain, he prays that his tongue will cleave to the roof of his mouth, rather than announce it. He asks for a greater audience. Four more people, their names unknown, are brought into the death chamber. The listeners shrink back into the shadows as the King speaks the awful words of warning.

> Long ago, when I was a youth in Normandy, I knew two monks, most holy men and dear to me. Many long years have passed since they were taken away from the cares and sorrows of this world. But now, in my trance, God hath sent them again to me to speak to me in His holy name.
>
> "Know," said they to me, "that they who hold the highest place in thy realm of England, the Earls, the Bishops, the Abbots, the men in Holy Orders of every rank, are not what they seem to be in the eyes of men.
>
> "In the eye of God they are but ministers of the fiend. Therefore hath God put a curse upon thy land; therefore hath He given thy land over into the hand of the enemy. Within a year and a day from thy death, shall fiends stalk through thy whole land, and shall harry it from one end to another with fire and sword and the hand of plunder."
>
> Then I said to them, "let me then show these things to my people in the name of God. Haply they will repent, and His loving-kindness will have mercy upon them. For He had mercy on the men of Nineveh, when they heard the voice of His threatening, and repented them of their evil ways."
>
> But they answered me, "they will not repent, neither shall the mercy of God come nigh unto them."
>
> Then I said, "what shall be the time or the way in which we may look for these things, your threatenings, to come to an end?"
>
> "In that day," they answered, "when a green tree shall be cut away from the midst of its trunk, when it shall be carried away for the space of three furlongs from its root, when, without the help of man, it shall join itself again to its trunk, and shall again put forth leaves and bear fruit in season. Then first shall be the time when the woes of England shall come to an end."

The awful words of doom, of fateful prophecy, die away. The listeners, overcoming their fears, draw closer to the bed. Stigand, worldly-wise and impatient, whispers to Harold that Edward's words are the babblings of an old and tired man. Edith shudders. Her husband's words have an uncanny semblance of truth. Stigand's appointment as archbishop remains uncanonical and unhallowed. Five popes have rejected it, refusing to him the pallium, the Church's recognition.

The full significance of the king's vision, if it was real and not cooked up when the evils he had predicted had come to pass, was lost upon his hearers. Edward's dying vision has been interpreted to mean that the crown would be transferred to usurpers during three reigns (the tree removed from its root for the space of three furlongs), those of Harold, William the Conqueror, and his son Rufus. The tree returned to its root when Henry I married Matilda, daughter of Margaret, Queen of Scotland, a descendant of Cerdic; it bore leaves in the persons of her children. The chronicler, William of Malmesbury, says that the birth of Henry's son Prince William (1101) was looked upon as the fulfillment of the prophecy. His death by drowning in the White Ship disaster in 1119 seemed to cut off all hopes, but it opened the way for a more elaborate fulfillment of the prophecy in the persons of his sister and her son Henry II.

Stigand leans over Edward. One question is prominent in the minds of his friends, he tells him. But Edward does not heed. He gives directions for his burial at the chosen spot within the hallowed walls of the Minster he has built, and he orders that his death be announced immediately, so that all the faithful may at once pray the Almighty for mercy upon him. Stigand presses the question: When he is gone, his body laid to rest, his soul gone to its reward, who shall fill the place he has so long filled upon earth? Who shall wear the crown of England?

Stigand and Harold wait in fearful expectation. The King is silent. His eyes turn to the men, and to the woman at his side. Slowly he raises and stretches forth his arm. He points to Harold. "To thee, Harold, I commend my kingdom, to hold it for my cousin William, to whom I have promised it," he whispers. The King's arm falls back on the bed. Harold stands aghast. The words he has feared have been spoken. His hope, that the King would nominate him as a patriotic duty, is shattered. Stigand shakes his arm. The Archbishop whispers "To thee, Harold, I *commit* my kingdom." You heard the King wrong, he suggests. The Queen nods assent. Harold looks around. The witnesses are too far away to have heard the King's whispered words. "I take you all to witness that the King has now given me the kingdom, and all the realm of England," he tells them, according to the compiler of the Norse sagas, Snorri Sturluson. The dying King is too far gone to overhear the muttered conclave. He expresses his last wishes. He asks Harold to protect his widow and his Norman friends, those whom, in his simplicity, he describes as the men who left their native land for love of him. He prays that those who wish to remain be permitted to do so, and those who desire to return to Normandy be allowed to go with their goods and wealth. He comforts the weeping Edith, "Fear not, I shall not die, but by God's grace I shall soon arise to better health." The end draws near. Stigand administers the last rites. Edward falls asleep, his cheeks like the rose, his beard like the lily, his hands fallen peacefully at his side.

This is an unusual interpretation of the Confessor's bequest of the throne. Many historians believe that, at the last minute, King Edward changed his mind and chose Harold to succeed him. He may have done so, but it seems more likely that he was coerced or his words falsely interpreted. The Norman chronicler, Benoît de St. More, states his opinion that the story of the King's bequest was Harold's invention. The Life of Edward the Confessor, the *Vita Edwardi Confessoris,* which may have been written shortly after his death, hints that the King's intelligence was impaired and that he was "broken with age and knew not what he said." William the Conqueror's most recent biographer, Professor David Douglas, suggests that the promise to Harold was "extracted under duress."

The news that the King is dead, and of his last fateful words, is carried to the Witan. From the courtyard of the palace the high quavering voice of a minstrel takes up his refrain, singing the praises of the king who is gone, the last son of the house of Cerdic.

The Witan is assembled in the great hall. It is the duty of the great men of England to name a new king. The situation is unprecedented. Long-standing custom requires that the king should be chosen from royal stock, preferably from members of the existing dynasty. But the next of kin did not succeed automatically. He might be considered too young, or otherwise unsuitable to rule in difficult times. It was thought wiser, more expedient, to choose the most vigorous kinsman of the late king, or at least a man of royal blood. That he might be a foreigner did not matter. When there was no obvious heir, the duty of filling the throne fell upon the Witan, the nation's leaders. The known wishes of the late King carried great weight, but the council was under no compulsion. The Witan could elect whom it wished, and the chosen man's right to the throne was as valid as if he had been born the eldest son of the late king.

The dying King had nominated Harold, the Witan is informed. Most of the magnates vote for Harold; they are his men. The Normans, the late King's favorites, may have spoken for William, urging the validity of Edward's promise and hinting at the sanctity of Harold's oath. Others may have suggested sending for the Aetheling Edgar. The northern earls, Edwin and Morcar, accept Harold grudgingly. Necessity rules the choice. There is no alternative, except passively to await the coming of Duke William or Harald Hardrada or both.

Two members of the Witan are sent to inform Harold, discreetly absent from their deliberations. One carries the simple workaday crown of England, the symbol of royal authority, while the other bears the great Axe of State, the gifts by which the people of England signify their king's election.

Harold stands to receive the deputation from the Witan. The moment for which he has longed and hoped has come. He is King. He knows that his reign may be dangerous. His election will stir two foreign princes to fury. One or both may try to take his crown. He cannot be certain that England will stand behind him, united in its own defense. He must accept the crown, if only to safeguard his own wealth and position. His oath to William, whatever its nature, is no bar to his acceptance. The choice of king is the Witan's, not his. England's crown is the gift of no man. Harold is 45 years old, in the prime of life. He is at the peak of his powers. He is not a man to shrink from responsibility and danger. He believes he is the only man who can steer England through the perils that lie ahead. Half Saxon and half Dane by birth, he thinks he can unite England against its foes.

As darkness falls, the new King keeps vigil by the bier of the old King. The lords and prelates prepare for the two ceremonies of the morrow. There is a king to be buried, a king to be crowned. That night, or early next morning, while it is still dark, King Edward is borne to his last rest. Dressed in his royal robes, crown on head, pilgrim's ring on finger, he is carried by torchlight procession into the Minster he built. His bier is carried on the shoulders of eight sturdy subjects; boys ringing bells walk on either side. Chanting priests, office books in hand, lead the way. Flickering torches light the gloom of the Minster's massive walls. The funeral cortege moves along the nave, passing long rows of tall pillars, to the prearranged spot beneath the mighty arches of the central tower where Edward's tomb has been hastily constructed. It glistens white in freshly hewn stone. Psalms are sung and masses said, and alms are scattered as prayers are offered for the soul of the departed. They will be sung and prayed for three hundred days. The lords and prelates hurry away to prepare for the even greater coronation ceremony on the Feast of Kings, the morning of Epiphany, when the new King and his people will exchange their mutual promises.

During the night, a lone horseman, cloaked to the eyes, steals out of London. He crosses the Thames and gallops south. He rides to a coastal port on one of the many creeks and harbors along the shores of Kent and Sussex. He takes ship to Normandy.

Two

The Oath

The ship from England sailed to a Norman port, probably Rouen. The messenger from London sought the duke who, he was told, was hunting in Quévilly Park nearby. Thither he went, crossing the Seine.

It was up the river Seine that the Norse Vikings had sailed in the ninth century. As they had done in England, they established small settlements; more Norsemen came and they extended their domain. Their leader, Rollo, made a pact with the King of France, whose vassal he became. In Normandy the Norsemen became absorbed into the people they vanquished, infusing a fresh virile impulse and adopting the culture of Latin Christendom. They became French in thought and language. They abandoned the sea and became mounted knights, the foremost land-warriors in Europe. They adopted the continental feudal system, whereby land was held in return for military service, creating thereby a powerful military machine.

Fifth in succession to Rollo, William succeeded to the Dukedom at the age of seven. To the disadvantages of minority rule was added the stigma of bastardy. The romantic circumstances of William's birth gave rise to a spate of legend and they make a good story, whatever their truth. When the duke Richard II died in 1026, he left two sons, the elder of whom, another Richard, succeeded him. The younger, Robert,

Count of the Heimois, rebelled against his brother and established himself at Falaise. He was no more than 18 years of age and he may have been even younger. One day, so the story goes, he was riding through the narrow dell which runs between the castle and the rugged heights beyond when he noticed, by the small stream which gurgles still beneath the castle's walls, a young girl. It was a case of love at first sight. Robert's eye caught the girl's beauty as she washed linen in the water, according to one version; as she danced by the brook, according to another. He called her and she came to him, standing by his side, taut with expectancy. Her name, she said, was Arlette and she was the daughter of Fulbert, a burgess of Falaise, a tanner by trade. Arlette's humble origin, cloaked by tactful reticence at the time, has given rise to considerable scholarly debate. Fulbert may have been a man who prepared corpses for burial, for the word describing his trade in the original French is of obscure meaning; it may be translated as either "tanner" or "embalmer." That Arlette's father was a tanner is suggested by two pieces of evidence: the stream by the castle was then, and continued to be for centuries, the abode of tanners, and when William was besieging Alençon in 1049, the defenders waved hides and skins from the walls to taunt him with his lowly birth. They could hardly have resisted the temptation to display a corpse on the ramparts. When William captured the town he ordered that their hands be cut off.

Count Robert took the girl to the castle where she reigned as his "wife," for the Norse custom of unsanctified unions or "Danish marriage," as it was called, survived conversion to Christianity. Arlette's son William was born either late in 1027 or early in 1028, after Robert had succeeded his brother. He did not legitimize his son by marriage with Arlette, and within a few years he married her off to Herlwin, Viscount of Conteville, to whom she bore two illustrious sons, the Conqueror's half-brothers, Eude, bishop of Bayeux, and Robert, Count of Mortain, his principal lieutenants in the invasion of England and the greatest beneficiaries of the conquest.

When William's father died while on a pilgrimage to the Holy Land, the barons, fearing the dangers of minority rule, paid unwilling homage to the boy who, nonetheless, was supported by the ducal family and by his souzerain, the King of France. The evils the barons had predicted quickly came to pass. Normandy became plunged in civil war. In the struggle for power two of William's principal supporters were murdered and he was saved from a like fate only by the foresight of Arlette's brother who fled at night with the boy, whom he hid in the cottages of the poor.

By 1041 the situation had become so serious that an attempt was made to introduce the Truce of God into the duchy. The Church declared that warfare, except against the Infidel, was repugnant to the principles of Christianity. It attempted to outlaw fighting between Christian Kings and their vassals, the barons great and small who claimed the right of waging war against anyone who was not their own overlord. The barons of Christendom rapturously greeted the proclamation of peace and fell upon their neighbors who were foolish enough to observe it. In vain the Church threatened ecclesiastical censure; it finally proposed a compromise. War was prohibited on certain days of the week and at the seasons of Advent, Lent, Easter and Pentecost. The Truce was proclaimed in Normandy at a council of Clergy and Laity convened at Caen in 1047 and for a time it was carefully observed. The satisfaction of private feuds was limited to three days in each week, from Monday through Wednesday; the disruption of order continued. Then anarchy turned into rebellion. It was a fateful year for William. As he attained his majority the barons of western Normandy rose in revolt. Again he barely escaped death. Fleeing from his enemies, he appealed for help to his overlord, the King of France, who came to his support, defeating the insurgents at the battle of Val-ès-Dunes, near Caen. William played a minor but significant part in the battle, performing prodigies of valor which enhanced his personal prestige. Charging, sword in hand, he attacked a veteran warrior, a famous knight, driving the steel into his body between throat and chest. This mighty strike, delivered with all William's immense strength, decided the turning point of the battle.

The victory strengthened William's position but it did not end his troubles. His supporters urged him to marry, stressing the advantages of an alliance with the French royal family. William's choice fell upon Matilda, daughter of Baldwin V, the Count of Flanders, a niece of King Henry. Baldwin was a key figure in European politics, a vassal of both France and the Holy Roman Empire, and Matilda carried the added advantage, if William's thoughts were turning already on Edward of England's childlessness, of lineal descent from King Alfred.

When William sought Matilda's hand in 1049 he encountered unexpected opposition from the Church, probably on the ground, though no intimate relationship can be traced, that William and Matilda were considered to come within prohibited degrees of blood. Whatever was the true nature of the impediment to their union, the couple were not wedded until 1051 or 1052, the Church still objecting. Somehow, probably by dubious means, William gained a powerful ally, Lanfranc, the famed prior of Bec, in his dispute with the Pope.

Lanfranc had come to Normandy in 1039 from Pavia in Italy. He was the son of a distinguished lawyer and he was both a Greek scholar and a man of deep theological learning. He established a school at Bec and his fame spread throughout Europe, where it was whispered that he denied the doctrines of the Church. Summoned to appear before the Papal Curia as a suspected heretic, he came away in 1050 with the reputation of being the most profound and orthodox scholar of the time.

Returning to Normandy at the height of the controversy about William's marriage, Lanfranc spoke against it, to the indignation of William, who ordered his banishment and the ravaging of the Abbey's lands. Lanfranc, on his journey into exile, met William, and he agreed to withdraw his opposition to the marriage, and to become William's champion at Rome for its recognition. What blandishments were required to secure this unscrupulous volteface is unknown, but when the time was ripe, Lanfranc journeyed to Rome to intercede with Pope Nicholas II, a more amenable prelate than his two predecessors, both stern and resolute popes. Lanfranc reached the Holy City at an opportune moment, in April 1059, when the Lateran Council was debating the alleged heresy of Berengar of Tours. Lanfranc appeared as the champion of orthodoxy, a position which may have influenced his appeal to Nicholas on behalf of William, for the recognition of whose marriage Lanfranc astutely argued. If the Papacy refused to recognise what was an accomplished fact, Matilda and her illegitimate children would be returned to her father, Baldwin of Flanders, whose injured pride could only lead to a family feud and the spilling of Christian blood, a situation which, Lanfranc urged, the Holy Father would deplore. The Prior's eloquence gained the day. Nicholas gave his dispensation in return for the promise that both William and Matilda would build and endow monastic foundations at Caen, a condition which they fulfilled, both buildings being consecrated before the Conquest. Lanfranc returned to Normandy to become the duke's foremost counsellor, and eventually the first Abbot of the great Abbey of St. Stephen at Caen.

William's marriage had another consequence. It linked him with Harold's brother Tostig who, in 1050, had married the half-sister of Baldwin V, the daughter of their father's old age. William had curbed his barons with the aid of his suzerain, the King of France and he had married the king's niece. Now King Henry turned against him, invading the duchy, one part of the French army advancing to relieve the fortress of Arques. The Normans sent a small force to intercept them. It turned and fled, drawing the impetuous Frenchmen into an ambush where those lying in wait fell upon them, an incident which establishes the Norman's use of the strategy of feigned flight in 1052, fourteen years before they may or may not have employed it with even more spectacular effect at the battle of Hastings. The bulk of the French army was destroyed by the Normans at Mortemer.

Between 1054 and 1064 William was constantly at war, but never after Mortemer was he faced with so formidable a threat to his independence, though the French King invaded again in 1057. Avoiding a pitched battle, William cut off and destroyed half the French army at Varaville, as it sought to escape across the river Dive.

Two years later King Henry died, and the same year, 1060, saw the death of William's principal rival for power in Northern France, Geoffrey Martel, the Count of Anjou. Fourteen years of incessant warfare had established William as the undisputed ruler of Normandy and the most powerful duke in France. The years of adversity had produced a man of iron will, ruthless, cunning, unscrupulous, a supreme realist who yet dreamed up a mad adventure. To be the greatest prince in Christendom was not enough for William. He desired a crown.

William's thoughts turned to England where the childless King was growing old, the Kingsman who had promised him the succession to the throne. What means Edward had adopted to convey his bequest to William is uncertain. The most plausible theory is that in 1051 he ordered the newly appointed Archbishop of Canterbury, the Norman prelate Robert of Jumièges, to break his return journey from Rome, where he went to receive his pallium from the pope, and call at Rouen.

That Edward adopted this means to inform the duke is more probable than that William came in person to England to receive the king's bequest. Only one manuscript of *The Anglo-Saxon Chronicle* says he did, stating he travelled with a long train of knights and returned home loaded with honors and gifts. *The Norman Chronicles* on the other hand, which were written within ten years of the Conquest, make no mention of such a momentous State visit at which their Duke was acknowledged as heir to the English throne. And it seems improbable that William would have left his duchy where he was still struggling for survival against formidable enemies.

William certainly believed that the promise had been made about the year 1051, for both the Norman chroniclers, William of Jumièges and William of Poitiers, report him as telling his troops before the battle of Hastings, that Edward had nominated him as his heir, that the promise had been confirmed on oath by the English Magnates and that Harold's father, Earl Godwine, had handed over his son Wulfnoth and his grandson Hakon as hostages for his good faith. One fact seems to confirm that Godwine did that; the English chronicler, Florence of Worcester, says that Wulfnoth and Hakon were held in custody by William from their youth, and that they were not resident in England is suggested by the absence of their names from Domesday as holding honors or lands in 1066.

The death of the Aetheling had removed the only legitimate rival to the throne. The glittering prize, the crown of England, appeared almost within William's grasp. One man stood in his way. As William rose to power in Northern France, so had Harold in England. Their positions were analogous; both were sub-kings, ambitious, powerful men, thirsty for even greater power. "Duke" Harold could ensure William's peaceful succession or make him fight for it. If we are to believe the Norman chroniclers, Harold tamely agreed to support William's succession on Edward's death.

The story of Harold's oath to William, sworn about the year 1064, is one of the most picturesque episodes in English history. Among contemporary chroniclers it is told exclusively by Normans. The English chroniclers are silent until the next century by which time a version had become current in which Harold's visit to Normandy was made to appear accidental, and the oath is obtained by fraud. This story is colored by the desire, probably, to explain the distasteful tradition that Harold had agreed to support William's succession to the throne. According to these late versions Harold sails from Bosham, a port in Southern England, on a pleasure cruise. He is wrecked on the coast of Ponthieu, taken prisoner by Count Guy and held for ransom, a predicament from which he is rescued by Duke William. Harold is forced to swear an oath on Holy relics which are concealed from his view. He is tricked into a declaration of the utmost sanctity.

The Bayeux Tapestry, the pictures of which were stitched within twenty years of the conquest, casts doubt on this version of the story, for Harold is depicted embarking with his men in three war galleys, and the Tapestry gives no hint of wreck, a picturesque detail which its designer would hardly have omitted.

The Norman chroniclers, William of Jumièges and William of Poitiers, state that Harold sailed to Normandy on a mission from King Edward to confirm in person his promise of the throne to William. Rescued from the hands of Count Guy by William, Harold, in the words of the monk of Jumièges, "performed fealty concerning the kingdom with many oaths." William of Poitiers reports William claiming that Edward, "finally sent me Harold himself to Normandy that in my presence he might personally take the oath which his father and others have sworn in my absence." Earlier in his narrative, William of Poitiers gives this description of the episode:

> About the same time, Edward, king of the English, who loved William as a brother or a son, established him as his heir with a stronger pledge than ever before. The king, who in his holy life showed his desire for a celestial kingdom, felt the hour of his death approaching, and wished to anticipate its inevitable consequences. He therefore despatched Harold to William in order that he might confirm his promise by an oath. This Harold was of all the king's subjects the richest and the most exalted in honour and power, and his brother and cousins had previously been offered as hostages in respect of the same succession. The king, indeed, here acted with great prudence in choosing Harold for this task, in the hope that the riches and authority of this magnate might check disturbance through out England if the people with their accustomed perfidy should be disposed to overturn what had been determined.

Whilst travelling upon this errand Harold only escaped the perils of the sea by making a forced landing on the coast of Ponthieu, where he fell into the hands of Count Guy, who threw him and his companions into prison. He may well have thought this a greater misfortune even than shipwreck, since among many peoples of the Gauls there was an abominable custom utterly contrary to Christian charity, whereby, when the powerful and rich were captured, they were thrown ignominiously into prison, and were maltreated and tortured even to the point of death, and afterwards sold as slaves to some magnate. When Duke William heard what had happened, he sent messengers at speed, and by prayers and threats he brought about Harold's honourable release. As a result Guy in person conducted his prisoner to the Castle of Eu, although he could at his pleasure have tortured or killed him, or sold him into slavery. Since, moreover, he did this very honourably without the compulsion of force or bribes, William in gratitude bestowed upon him rich gifts of land and money, and then took Harold with proper honour, to Rouen. This was the chief city of the Norman duchy, and there William sumptuously refreshed Harold with splendid hospitality after all the hardships of his journey. For the duke rejoiced to have so illustrious a guest in a man who had been sent to him by the nearest and dearest of his friends; one moreover, who was in England second only to the king, and who might prove a faithful mediator between him and the English.

When they had come together in conference at Bonneville, Harold in that place swore fealty to the duke, employing the sacred ritual recognised among Christian men. And as is testified by the most truthful and most honourable men who were there present, he took an oath of his own free will in the following terms: firstly that he would be the representative of duke William at the court of his lord, king Edward, as long as the king lived; secondly that he would employ all his influence and wealth to ensure that after the death of king Edward the kingdom of England should be confirmed in the possession of the duke; thirdly that he would place a garrison of the duke's knights in the Castle of Dover and maintain these at his own care and cost; fourthly that in other parts of England at the pleasure of the duke who would maintain garrisons in other Castles and make complete provision for their substenance. The duke on his part who before the oath was taken had received ceremonial homage from him, confirmed to him at his request all his lands and dignities. For Edward in his illness could not be expected to live much longer.

The most accurate version of the incident, probably, is that depicted in the Tapestry. William and Harold are at Bayeux, the caption stating WHERE HAROLD MADE AN OATH TO WILLIAM. William is seated on an elevated throne; Harold stands bareheaded with his hands extended between two chests of relics, which are openly displayed. There is no suggestion of subterfuge and no hint of the nature of the oath. The only clue is derived from the following scenes in which Harold is shown on his return to England being received by King Edward, whose countenance is disturbed and sorrowful, and interpretation of the scene which has been taken to suggest that the King had warned Harold against being tricked by William and that events had proved him right. Harold, it is assumed, went to Normandy, with Edward's reluctant permission, to secure the release of the hostages. He returns without them, having been compelled to swear an oath to support William's candidature.

In the more fanciful account of Wace, who lived at Bayeux and who may or may not have known the Tapestry, the relics are concealed and Harold's hand trembles and his flesh quivers as he swears to take William's daughter to wife, to give his sister in marriage to a Norman noble and to deliver up England to the duke on the death of Edward. After the oath is sworn, William lifts a pall from the chest, exposing the Holy relics, and Harold is sorely alarmed.

Thus, dismissing the later "pleasure cruise" explanation for Harold's voyage, we have three possible reasons why Harold visited Normandy; to engage to marry William's daughter, to obtain the release of the hostages, or to confirm the king's promise in person. Harold, it seems, can hardly have been so naive as to imagine that William would give up his brother and nephew, the only hold he had on him. Harold, being then unmarried, could have contracted to marry one of William's daughters; their extreme youth would have been no bar to eventual consummation.

Harold, it seems certain, was sent to Normandy to confirm the King's promise of the succession. He never denied swearing an oath to William: he claimed it had been obtained by fraud and he stated, correctly, that it was invalid, because he had no right to dispose of England's crown. That was the Witan's responsibility. It is possible that William hoped that Harold would break the oath, thus providing him with a powerful weapon against the perjurer.

William now believed, or feigned to believe, that Harold would support his succession to the throne promised by King Edward. William had also seen something of his rival. The Tapestry depicts William's campaigning in Britanny, where he is accompanied by Harold whose part in the expedition is emphasized; impetuously risking his life, he drags several Normans from the quicksands of the Couesson river. From this incident, William learned that Harold was a brave and impetuous soldier, prone to rashness.

As the months went by, William lived in fervent expectancy that he would soon be King of England. Toward the close of 1065, he was told that the old king lay dying.

Three

The Plan

The messenger, one of the Normans resident in England, the emissary perhaps of the Norman Staller Robert Fitz-Wymarc, went to Quévilly park where he found the duke hunting. William, records Wace, took the news of Edward's death and of Harold's coronation badly; it plunged him into anger and despair, from which he was aroused by his old friend, the Seneschal William Fitz-Osbern who urged him to cross the sea and avenge himself upon the usurper.

William pondered the wrongs done him by Harold. He knew that he must fight to win the crown of England. He knew, even if he would not admit it, that Edward's promise was worthless, that Harold's oath was meaningless, that his kinship to the late King did not entitle him to the succession. If he understood English law and custom, and William attended to such details, he knew that under no conceivable theory of succession was he the legitimate heir. William pretended to believe that the Witan should have elected him king and that Harold should have supported his candidacy. Harold the perjurer, the oath-breaker, the blasphemer, had usurped the crown that was rightfully William's crown, the kingship William so ardently desired, that he could yet win by the sword. William laid his plans, a task in which he was ably assisted by the scholarly Lanfranc, the Italian theologian with the supple mind.

William, like the professional burglar, knew that however much he schemed and planned, in the end he would still have to scale the drainpipe, force the window, climb into the building and overcome the landlord. To win England he had to gather a great army, build a fleet, cross the Channel and force Harold to fight a decisive battle. That would be no easy task, for the King of England was an experienced general, commanding a powerful army and capable of mobilizing an efficient fleet. To conquer England would be a tremendous undertaking, far beyond the power of Normandy. It would be a dangerous enterprise in which, while trying to win a crown, he might lose his duchy. Carefully, William calculated the risks. Harold, he knew from personal observation, was an impetuous soldier, prone to rashness.

William and Lanfranc conferred. The Prior was apprehensive of the feasibility of the plan, fearful of its outcome and dubious of its morality. The invasion of England would be a war of wanton aggression, exactly the type of warfare that the Church condemned and had devised the Truce of God to forbid, he warned. William had an answer to the prelate's objections. The invasion of England would be a crusade, a holy war to punish the oath-breaker, to avenge Harold's insult to God. He would lead an army to take the kingdom that Harold had treacherously seized, a band of devoted missionaries to reform the evils and abuses into which the Church in England had lapsed. The appointment of Stigand as Archbishop of Canterbury had been denied apostolic blessing, he observed. The Holy Father would be pleased, not angered, if he, William, a devout son of the Church, subdued England and reformed the English Church. He would be the champion of Christendom, and Lanfranc would make an excellent archbishop. Lanfranc grasped the point. The Holy Father, he agreed, might be persuaded to give the enterprise his blessing.

Lanfranc's hesitancy quickly evaporated. William had to win all Christendom to his cause, he urged. The pen could be as mighty as the sword. He had to arouse the conscience of Europe against Harold the blasphemer. To gain support and much-needed volunteers to swell his army, it was necessary to present his war against Harold, not as a private quarrel, but as a crusade against a usurper. He had to cloak wanton aggression in the guise of holy war. His claim to England's throne had to sound legitimate, which was not difficult to manage in Europe, where the doctrine of popular election was little understood and appeared unnatural to hereditary rulers. He had to put Harold in the wrong. When William had defeated and killed Harold, the Witan would have no choice but to elect William king. He would reign by law and custom, not by war and conquest. His war would be against the usurper, to free England from Harold, the enemy of God.

William and his adviser listed the ingredients for success. He had to win the support of the Pope and of all Christendom, gain the backing of his own barons and secure his duchy while he was overseas.

The first move was obvious, and William made it quickly. He sent an embassy to England, calling upon Harold to fulfill his oath and relinquish the crown to him. If he declined, William, Duke of Normandy, would come against him in arms to support his rights. In his answer, Harold quoted one of the best known axioms of English law: "If the oath or vow which a maiden under her father's roof, made concerning her person without the knowledge of her parents, was adjudged invalid, how much more invalid must that oath be which he made concerning the whole kingdom and without the knowledge of the nation." His oath to William had been obtained by compulsion and fraud, and therefore it was void. To break it was less evil than to keep it. He had been named King of England by the voice of the people, and the people of England alone could deprive him of the throne.

William laid his case before the Pope. On Lanfranc's advice, he directed it to the particular attention of an up-and-coming young prelate, an official of the Papal Curia, Archdeacon Hildebrand by name. He, Lanfranc believed, possessed the most astute mind in Rome, an estimate confirmed by Hildebrand's later election to the papacy. As Pope Gregory VII, he became the most famous of all medieval popes.

The papacy, Lanfranc believed, would be flattered by a request to adjudicate the affairs of an earthly kingdom, to judge the succession to a temporal throne. Such a request from a reigning prince would be a signal demonstration of the growing power of the papacy and of religion itself. It would also be a tribute to rule by law and order, by arbitration rather than by resort to the sword. But an appeal to Rome would set a dangerous precedent. William understood the Prior's meaning. If the Bishop of Rome was invited to determine who was the lawful heir to the crown of England, there was the inherent danger that future popes would claim the right to interfere in the temporal affairs of the kingdom. The blast of the divine trumpet that would declare Harold a usurper, and William the lawful heir, could be a forerunner of even mightier blasts, the echoes of which might reverberate down the ages. William saw the danger, but he believed himself strong enough to overcome it. Papal support helped William to win his crown; he thus created a rod for the backs of his successors.

The strength of his army lay in his Norman barons and their knights, William knew. Again difficulties arose. Under the feudal system of military service in return for land tenure, every baron owed annually forty days' military service, each leading a contingent of knights, men-at-arms and bowmen, according to his degree. But his duty to the lord was confined to France. The Duke of Normandy could not force his lieges to perform service overseas. If they followed him to England, they would have to go as volunteers. To induce his barons to volunteer, William had to arouse their sympathy for his cause and whet their greed by splendid promises of rewards and plunder. Normandy was seething with lusty, hot-headed knights, anxious for adventure and renown, young men seeking land of their own.

Early in March, William called a conference of his most trusted counsellors, the great barons and prelates of Normandy, men of his own blood, the friends of his youth, the faithful vassals who had fought and conquered at his side. They included his half brothers Robert, Count of Mortain, and Eude, Bishop of Bayeux; William Fitz-Osbern, the Seneschal; Eude de Capello, the husband of his half sister; Richard d'Evreux, grandson of Duke Robert the Fearless; Roger de Montgomery, a great friend, and Walter Giffard, Roger de Villes, Roger de Beaumont, Hugh de Grandmesnil, Hugh de Montfort, William de Warenne, powerful, ambitious men, strong in arm and stout of heart. The council gathered at its sovereign's bidding. William told the great barons of his design, how Harold had seized his rightful crown, and that, if they approved, he would cross the sea to avenge himself. The great barons said they would go with him; they would pledge their lands if necessary, but they could not speak for others, the hundreds of lesser barons of Normandy. The Duke, they advised, should summon them to assembly.

The Duke's marshals rode forth to summon his array. From all parts of the duchy the barons rode to the ancient town of Lillebonne, the appointed trysting place, where William had built a castle. In its stately hall the nobles of Normandy gathered to hear their lord's proposal. It was a gathering without precedent. Never before had a duke of Normandy called a "parliament" of his people. William laid his case before them. Harold had cheated him and stolen the kingdom to which Edward had made William heir. Without their help he could do nothing. He took their zeal for granted, but would they go with him to avenge himself and God upon Harold?

The enterprise was sheer madness, declared many of the barons. The Norman army was not strong enough to conquer England, and Normandy possessed no fleet. Harold could mobilize a far greater army, and he could control the Channel with a powerful navy capable of destroying the invasion before a landing could be made. It was an enterprise beyond even the power of a Roman emperor. William waved aside their protests: England was torn by dissension and its vaunted army was antiquated, unfamiliar with the newest techniques of warfare, armed and trained only to repel undisciplined raiders. The Normans were ever victorious; they had proved invincible in Europe. They would not go alone. Volunteers, veterans of a dozen campaigns, would join the crusade against the usurper Harold. William stressed the advantages to be gained, the rich plunder, land for younger sons, brothers and cousins, and dowries for daughters. The barons asked for time to consider.

The assembly broke up into little parties, groups of arguing, gesticulating men surrounding speakers, here five, there fifteen, here forty, there thirty, sixty, a hundred. They argued about what they would say; they murmured and complained, reviving ancient grievances. Some said they were willing to cross the sea with the Duke; others said they were too poor or the hazards too great. "Some said they would go, others would not, and there was great contention amongst them," records Wace.

The feeling of the meeting was definitely against the enterprise, William was informed. He sent William Fitz-Osbern to cajole the assembly. They owed William service for their fiefs, he advised the barons. What they owed they ought to render with all their might. "Wait not for him to beseech you; ask him for no respite, but go forward at once and offer him even more than you can perform," he implored. "Let not the Duke have cause to complain, or miss his undertaking on your account." William's jealous temper would not brook disappointment. "Take care that he has not to say that this expedition failed through you," warned the Seneschal. "We fear the sea, and we are not bound to serve beyond it," pleaded the barons. "Speak for us, for you know our minds," they asked Fitz-Osbern.

Fitz-Osbern led the barons to the Duke. But he did not speak their minds. He set out to stampede the meeting. "Sire, sire, look around. There is no people under heaven that so love their lord, or would do so much for his honour, as the people you have; and much should you love and protect them. They say that to advance you, they will swim through the sea, or throw themselves into the raging fire; you may trust them much, for they have served you long, and followed you at great cost, and they will willingly continue to serve you. If they have hitherto done well, they will hereafter do yet better. They will pass with you over the sea, and double their service. He who should bring twenty knights will cheerfully bring forty; he who should serve with thirty will now serve with sixty; and he who owes a hundred will willingly bring two hundred. For myself, I will in good love bring to my lord, in his need, sixty ships, well furnished and charged with fighting men."

The Seneschal's speech was greeted with loud murmurs. The barons were aghast at the great promises he had made on their behalf, for which he had no warranty. Their spokesman had pledged them to engagements that had never entered their minds. Loud shouts of dissent rang through the hall. The barons feared that doubling their services would turn into charges on their fiefs and would become customary dues. The clamor rose higher and louder; no one could hear himself speak, and no one would listen to reason. The confusion prevented a vote being taken.

Fitz-Osbern's rash promise had destroyed all hope of consent. His subterfuge had only enraged the barons. The Duke sought to turn his Seneschal's hazardous experiment to advantage. He sent for the barons, one by one, to cajole each separately, unsupported by membership of a crowd. Cunningly, he took it for granted that each man was willing to go with him, pretending that the only argument was the amount of service each would render. If each doubled his service of his own accord, he pledged himself that in future none should be called on for service beyond the custom. No precedent would be established if the barons brought more men than their due, promised William.

Skillfully, adroitly, William played on each man's vanity and greed.

He recalled past incidents of war; he spoke of daring deeds and great occasions when they had fought side by side. He hinted at the spoils and plunder, the lands each and all would gain in England, the great heritage they would pass on to their children and to their children's children. The magic of William's personality prevailed. Although he had not gained the collective vote of the assembly, he had obtained the personal promise of each of his barons to serve as a volunteer in the army of conquest. As the barons vowed their men and ships, William's clerks noted each promise in a book. William's half brother Eude gave 100 ships; his half brother Robert, 120. And so the tally went on. Ordericus Vitalis lists the guarantees:

William Fitz-Osbern	60
Hugh d'Avranche	60
Hugh de Montfort	50
Bishop Remigius	1
Nicholas, Abbot of St. Ouen	20
Robert d'Eu	60
Fulk le Boîteux	40
Gerald Dapifer	40
Richard, Comte d'Evreux	80
Roger de Montgomery	60
Roger de Beaumont	60
Walter Giffard	30
Queen Matilda	1

The whole might of Normandy was not sufficient to conquer England, William knew. With his barons won, he turned to invite volunteers from outside Normandy, from all Christendom. He called upon his neighbors, the Bretons, the Mansels and the Angevins, the men of Poitou and Boulogne and Aquitaine, to come with him in his need. To those who asked for land, he promised land. To many he promised other rewards, good pay and rich gifts. Soldiers of fortune flocked to William's standard, landless knights, sturdy men-at-arms and archers. From them he formed a great mercenary army, an innovation that became the basis of all European armies by 1300.

William sought even stronger allies. He showed (in Wace's words) to King Philip of France, his lord, how for good cause and for his honor's sake, he was about to cross the sea against Harold, who had

broken faith and defrauded him. The Duke went to speak with the King at the Abbey of St. Germer near Gournay in France and only a few miles from the Norman frontier. He described his situation and promised that if the King would aid him, and if through that aid he should win his crown, he would hold England of him and would serve him for it as his vassal.

The King of France refused to aid William. The king's advisers counselled him not to allow the already too powerful Duke to further strengthen himself by adding to his strength the wealth and great force of England. If he did, they said, the King of France would never have peace in his life; he ought rather to think of preventing William from going to England. The Duke sought his aid only for his own interest. "He serves you but little now, and he will serve you still less when he shall have conquered England. The more he has, the less he will do for you," warned the boy king's counsellors.

When the Duke heard of this advice he was wrothful, and he told the King: "Sire, I will go and will do the best I can. If God please, I will seek my right. If I win it, which God grant, you shall do me no harm; if the English are able to defend themselves so that I fail, I shall not lose heart or head on that account. All things shall be set in order; my children shall have my land, and you shall not take advantage of them; whether I die or live, whatever befall me, I fear the threat of no man."

Rebuffed by the King of France, William sent an embassy to his father-in-law Baldwin, Count of Flanders, asking him to join his crusade. The Count, one of the most powerful men in Europe, replied cautiously. If he were to give aid, what share of England and what division of the spoil would he have? The Duke was equally cautious, so that at this distance of time it is difficult to understand his reply. He would discuss it with his barons, he said, and would report by letter what they advised. Then he took a small piece of parchment, which had neither letter nor writing upon it, sealed it with wax, blank as it was, wrote upon the label that the Count should have such part of England as the letter within stated and sent it to Bruges by a cunning varlet who had long been with him. The varlet delivered it to the Count, who broke the seal and looked at the letter within. When he saw nothing, he showed it to the varlet, who told him in an offhand way, "Naught is there and naught shall thou have. Therefore look for nothing." If God pleased, the Duke would conquer England for himself, the messenger told the Count.

William failed to gain the active support of his father-in-law, who may have refused his help because of his duty to the boy king of France whose guardian he was, but he allowed Flemish knights to volunteer for William's army, and he gave his son-in-law "sagacious counsel," states William of Malmesbury. Baldwin, it seems, helped William by furnishing Harold with false information about the strength of the Norman host.

William achieved several diplomatic successes. The Holy Roman Emperor Henry IV, issued an edict authorizing his vassals to volunteer for the Duke's army, and William secured the neutrality of Denmark, whose King, Sweyn, Harold's cousin, agreed not to interfere and even promised to send a body of troops, which does not seem to have materialized.

Most important of all, William's embassy to Rome prospered. He sent several clerks (prelates) under the leadership of Gilbert, Archdeacon of Lisieux, to the "Apostle," the title by which the Pope was then known, telling how Harold had broken his oath and lied and how he had refused to render to William the kingdom Edward had promised and Harold himself had guaranteed on oath. On William's behalf the embassy asked that Harold's perjury be punished according to the rules of Holy Church, and it promised that if by God's will William should conquer England, he would hold the kingdom of St. Peter and do service for it to none but God. The problem of England's kingship was debated in conclave. The Pope, Alexander II, expressed his gratification that William was prepared to acknowledge that the King of England had a superior on earth. But when Hildebrand dwelt on the benefits to the Church, there was a storm of protest. Many cardinals rejected his arguments with horror. It was not for the Church of Christ to partake in deeds of blood and violence and to sanction claims that could be enforced only by slaughter. The horrors of war were permissible when the interests of the Church were at stake, countered Hildebrand. Never before had the pope been given such an opportunity to win authority over a great kingdom. William's appeal to Rome created an important precedent by which Rome could claim the disposal of every crown in Christendom.

The Pope, after considering the matter, granted William's request, making a decree that recognized William as the lawful claimant and blessing his cause with costly gifts; a precious gonfalon (a consecrated banner) and a holy relic, a ring under the stone of which lay one of St. Peter's hairs. "With these tokens," records Wace, "the Apostle commanded, and in God's name granted to William, that he should conquer England and hold it of St. Peter." Harold was not represented, and his case was lost by default.

William had won the battle for men's minds. The Holy Father supported his cause. From all over Europe men flocked to join his crusade against the usurper, many of them near-brigands anxious to obtain the Church's absolution for acts of robbery and slaughter. A band of Norman knights set out to ride from faraway Sicily, and the King of Spain promised the Duke a noble horse. Eustace, Count of Boulogne, eager to avenge himself on the people of Dover with whom he had had a fracas, sent a message that he would come.

William was not yet done. He launched what we would now call a "smear" campaign against Harold, raking up past grievances, among them the unfounded claim that Harold had murdered the Aetheling Edward whom, it was alleged, he had enticed from Hungary in order to remove the only legitimate successor to the throne.

William's "hate" campaign incensed the men of Europe against Harold; from Germany, Italy, Flanders, France and Brittany, bands of volunteers set out to join the Duke of Normandy in his crusade against England. In Normandy the woods and valleys rang with the sound of axes, adzes, anvils and hammers, as the barons and their men cut timber with which to build the vessels they had promised to their lord and forged the lances, swords and arrows with which to conquer England.

William had thrown down his challenge to Harold. While his barons prepared for the great enterprise, he set out to secure his dukedom from attack while he was away. In this task fortune played into his hands. His old enemies were dead; the King of France was a minor, his counsellors too divided to wage war against the powerful Duke; Anjou, Normandy's hereditary enemy, was torn by a war of succession. William could go in peace to undertake perhaps the most perilous and reckless adventure upon which any ruler has ever set out.

Now, in the words of Wace, while these things were doing, a great star appeared, shining for fourteen nights, with three long rays streaming toward the south. "Such a star," he says, "as is wont to be seen when a kingdom is about to change its king." Those who discoursed of the stars called it a "comet," he states in his chronicle.

Four

The Warrior

The news of Edward's death and of Harold's coronation was carried to Harald Hardrada, King of Norway. The vast quantities of English coins, including those of Edward the Confessor, found in the northern counties suggest that there was considerable trade between England and Norway, and the peoples of northern England and Scandinavia were of the same racial stock. They spoke the same language or at least could understand one another, as is shown by the conversation between a Norwegian fugitive and a Yorkshire peasant recorded in the saga of Snorri Sturluson after the battle of Stamford Bridge.

Hardrada, as we may call him, believed that he was the rightful King of England, by virtue of the pact made by his predecessor, King Magnus, with Harthacanute. To preserve the empire of Canute, they had agreed that, should either die without direct heirs, the survivor should inherit the kingdoms of the other. When Harthacanute died in 1042, Magnus was forestalled in England by the speedy election of Edward, and he was too preoccupied in Denmark, fighting Sweyn, Canute's nephew and Harthacanute's cousin for the crown, to plan the invasion of England until 1045. Then a flare-up of the war in Denmark prevented him from sailing. Magnus died in 1047, and his claim to England's throne was inherited by his successor, his uncle Harald Sigurdsson, who earned the nickname "Hardrada," the hard-ruler or tyrant. He sent a fleet to raid the English coast, but he was too busy fighting to oust Sweyn from Denmark to revive his family's dubious claim until a respite in 1058 allowed him to send his son, who raided the English coast with a large fleet that he had collected in the Hebrides and Ireland. The time was not yet ripe for full-scale invasion.

At 51, Hardrada was the most famous warrior of the age. In his youth all Europe had rung with his exploits. After recovering from wounds sustained at the battle of Stiklestad, Hardrada fled Norway and travelled to Russia, gaining the friendship of Grand Duke Jaroslaf of Novgorod and the love of his daughter Elizabeth. The young Norwegian prince still had his fortune to make, and he set out with a few companions for Byzantium, the capital of the decaying Eastern Roman Empire. He reached the city on the Bosporus during the period known as the "reigns of the husbands of Zoë," the empress who alternatively exalted and murdered her lovers. According to the Norse sagas, Hardrada, with his long blond hair and gigantic frame, made a sensation in Byzantium, where he was appointed commander of the Varangian Guard, recruited from volunteers from Scandinavia.

Allowing for the natural pride of the Norwegians in their hero, it appears that Hardrada infused new life into the Imperial army, which was waging war against the Saracens throughout the eastern Mediterranean. He led, or at least co-commanded, an expedition that attacked the Saracens and their Christian allies in Sicily. Between 1038 and 1040, he besieged and reduced several castles, some by direct assault, others by subterfuge. One he entered by a tunnel dug beneath the walls, emerging in a storeroom and taking the defenders by surprise. Balked before the walls of another, held by Christians, he feigned death. His sorrowing friends besought the garrison to grant their chief burial in consecrated ground. The good monks welcomed the opportunity to acquire the tomb of so illustrious a warrior. Slowly the mourning Varings bore their leader's body up the slope to the castle's gate. The minstrels walked behind, singing Hardrada's dirge. The monks stood in the open gateway, awaiting the corpse. Dropping their burden, the Varings drew swords from beneath their cloaks. With Hardrada at their head, they rushed the gate, killing the monks and holding it long enough for their companions to run up and take the castle.

During his campaign in Sicily, Hardrada encountered the Norman knights, exiles from their homeland, who had carved out a kingdom for themselves. They were horse-riding soldiers who had learned and adopted Byzantine military techniques, men of whom we shall hear more later.

Hardrada is reported to have carried the war against the infidel into North Africa and, on its conclusion, to have made a pilgrimage to the Holy Sepulchre, clearing from the path the many robbers who beset the road to Jerusalem, preying upon Christian pilgrims. He lavished gifts on the tomb of Christ and bathed in the River Jordan before returning to Byzantium, where he found that his fame had earned him enemies at court. The Empress, who may have had an eye on the stalwart Norwegian, refused him the hand of her niece, the Princess Maria, and Hardrada's freedom was placed in jeopardy. His reaction was typical. Abducting the Princess, Hardrada and his companions sought to escape in two galleys. Their course to the Black Sea was blocked by the great chain strung across the Bosporus. As the galley's keels grated on its giant links, Hardrada ordered his warriors to the stern; the rowers lay on their oars. The bows lifted, the oarsmen pulled and the warriors scampered to the prow. With a grinding jerk, the galleys grated over the chain. Free to pursue his voyage, Hardrada put the Princess ashore and sailed to Russia, eventually reaching Novgorod, where he married Grand Duke Jaroslav's daughter, taking her to Norway with his great block of gold, his loot from Byzantium.

Hardrada was welcomed by his nephew Magnus, who agreed to share his royal dignity in return for half Hardrada's treasure, which he needed to prosecute his war against Denmark. The friendship between the royal kinsmen was short-lived, however. Hardrada's greed and tyrannical rule alienated the Norwegians, and for a time he took the part of Sweyn. On Magnus's death Hardrada changed his tactics. Intercepting the late King's dying message to Sweyn acknowledging his right to the Danish throne, Hardrada, as full King of Norway, laid claim to Denmark. An incident recorded in the sagas for the year 1049 demonstrates Hardrada's resourcefulness. He had been ravaging the coasts of Denmark, whence he had abducted a number of high-born women. Not expecting pursuit, the Norwegian fleet sailed home leisurely. One foggy morning Hardrada found that his ship and several others had become separated from the main fleet. A sudden flash of light sparkled high in the mist. His men were mystified, but Hardrada at once recognized the danger. "The Danish fleet is upon us; that which shines are the golden dragon heads which flash in the morning sun," he announced. As the powerful Danish fleet emerged from the mist, both resistance and flight seemed hopeless. The Norwegian ships were heavy with plunder, their wooden hulls swollen with water. The Danish galleys bore down, their crews shouting triumphantly. Hardrada ordered his men to affix all the precious things they could find to logs and planks and to throw them overboard. The recovery of the treasures delayed the Danes and the Norwegian ships drew away. The Danes caught up, but valuable distance had been gained. Next, Hardrada ordered that all the ships' provisions, the carcasses of cattle and pigs, bags of oatmeal and barrels of beer, be jettisoned. Again the Danes delayed to collect the loot. The Norwegians rowed on slowly. Within an hour the Danes had caught up. In desperation, Hardrada commanded that the greatest treasure of all, the Danish high-born women, be tied to barrels and cast into the sea. But not all together—he sent them off at intervals, and the pursuers, seeing their wives and daughters stretching out their arms, seeking rescue, stopped again. The rescues took a long time, as each woman had been securely shackled to the barrels. Thus records the saga, "Hardrada escaped and Sweyn cursed his ill-luck."

Hardrada showed his capability for improvisation again during an expedition to Denmark in 1060. Having defeated Sweyn in battle, the Norwegians sailed into a narrow fjord looking for plunder. Reassembling his fleet, Sweyn blockaded its narrow mouth. Seeing that he was caught in a trap, Hardrada sought another way out. At the far end, a narrow isthmus separated the fjord from the sea. Dragging his ships overland, he refloated them and sailed away, leaving Sweyn hopefully watching the empty cage.

Realizing that he could not drive Sweyn from the throne of Denmark without support from within the Danish kingdom, Hardrada made peace in 1064. A man of restless ambition, he could not remain inactive. The news of Edward's death came at an opportune moment. Norway was filled with lusty fighting men, warrior-oarsmen who made their living from the spoils of war. Hardrada saw his chance to revive the empire of Canute, to become Emperor of the North. One factor only was lacking to settle his decision. Could he be sure of support within the kingdom he sought to conquer?

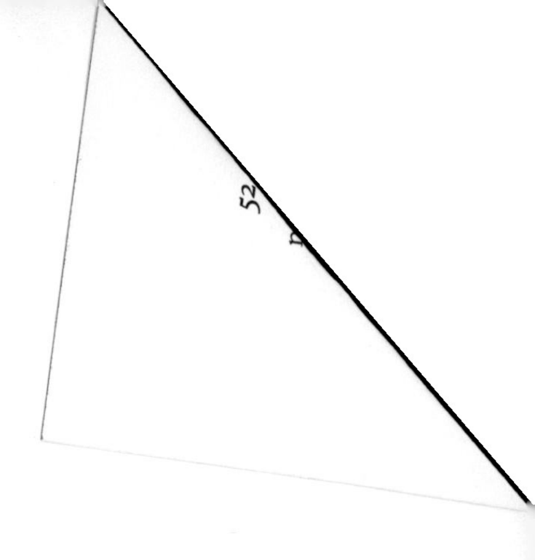

Five

The Hairy Star

Within a few weeks of his coronation, King Harold knew that the Duke of the Normans would come in arms to assert his claim to the throne. Hardrada, he guessed, would also invade. Within a few months, England might be attacked, perhaps simultaneously from north and south, by the two greatest warriors of the age. His brother Tostig would certainly support one or the other of his enemies, and both Tostig and Hardrada would seek supporters in northern England. Harold could have been in no doubt of the double danger he faced, a two-front war in Yorkshire and Sussex at a time when he was still uncertain of northern support. He felt justifiably confident of defeating either William or Hardrada, but he could not repel both invaders without the help of Earls Edwin and Morcar. They had not actively opposed his election, and the seal of northern approval had been given in his consecration by Eldred, Archbishop of York who, rather than the uncanonical Stigand, probably had performed the holy rite of coronation. But Harold needed more than passive approval from the two northern Earls. He set out to gain their active allegiance. No king of England had travelled farther north than Shrewsbury since 1017, when Canute had marched his army through Northumbria. In the late winter of 1066 Harold rode to York, accompanied only by a small bodyguard and taking with him Wulfstan, the saintly Bishop of Worcester. At a meeting of the northern magnates held at York, Harold argued the necessity of unity in the face of the dangers that threatened each and all. Cunningly, he stressed that Hardrada probably, and William possibly, would be supported by Tostig, eager to regain his Northumbrian earldom and anxious to pay off old scores. Harold's marriage about that time to Edith, widow of King Griffith of Wales and sister to Edwin and Morcar, indicates that his plea for unity was approved. Dire necessity only could have overcome the repugnance of the sons of Leofric to an alliance with a member of the family that had for thirty years ruthlessly pursued power at their expense. Harold's dynastic marriage is a clear pointer to the alarm that the invasion threats caused early in 1066.

Harold returned to London free to concentrate on the defense of southern England against William, which he clearly considered the major threat. Harold may well have believed, as did many of the Norman barons, that a successful invasion of England was beyond the power of a Roman emperor, but his actions show that he took the threat seriously. Early in his reign Harold expelled many of the Normans who had settled in England. But he did not dispossess them all or despoil them of their wealth; several were allowed to remain. Men like William, Bishop of London; Staller Robert Fitz-Wymarc; and perhaps Hugolin, the Treasurer, and Reginbald, the Chancellor, remained, for the Normans made no claim that these men had been deprived of their offices. Harold, unless he was misled by their protestations of loyalty, must have believed they offered no threat to his security. One, at least, of these men acted as William's spy.

With the North secure as long as the invasion threat lasted, and the South controlled by the King, who retained the earldom of Wessex, and by his two brothers, Gyrth and Leofwine, the earls of East Anglia and Kent and Essex, Harold's optimism increased. He had nothing to fear from Wales, whose two kings he had defeated and slain in a prolonged war that had ended in 1065. Scotland, on the other hand, had some potential nuisance value, for its king, Malcolm, was sworn blood brother to Tostig, who had helped him regain the throne usurped by Macbeth, the murderer of his father Duncan.

Little is known of Harold's rule during his nine months' reign. *The Anglo-Saxon Chronicle* records only that he "met with little quiet as long as he ruled the kingdom." In his panegyric to Harold, Florence of

Worcester says, "he began to abolish unrighteous laws, to establish righteous ones, to reverence Bishops, Abbots, Monks and churchmen of every sort, to show himself pious, lowly and affable to all good men, and to be the enemy of all evil-doers." He bade his earls, sheriffs and thegns seize all thieves, robbers and disturbers of the peace, while he labored for the defense of the land.

During the early months of his reign, Harold issued a voluminous currency, ordering the striking of coins bearing the word *pax* on one face and the image of the King wearing the Imperial Diadem on the other. These coins were to be struck at forty-four minting places, but the moneyers had to obtain their dies from London, thus ensuring central control. It seems possible that Harold's monetary policy was designed to revitalize trade, which had stagnated due to difficulties of distribution, for the volume of production and exchange was low and taxation was high. England was the only country in Europe to levy a special war tax to support a professional army. At a time when other powers raised armies through the feudal obligation of service in return for land, England paid its soldiers and sailors to fight.

The English army that fought at Hastings is often described as an undisciplined rabble, the savage retainers of barbaric earls and thegns, an antiquated force equipped with obsolete weapons and trained in the tactics of a past age, the product of a system sunk in stagnation and decay. On the contrary, the Anglo-Saxon army was the equal, and probably the superior, of any contemporary force, and the English navy was unique and justly famed.

The army was composed of three forces, the housecarls, the select fyrd and the great fyrd. The housecarls, introduced by Canute, were professional soldiers, a standing army of about three thousand men, an elite corps, governed by an elaborate code of conduct and organized on the lines of the Varangian Guard of the Byzantine emperors. They were paid in peace and war, and they were trained to fight on both land and sea. Equipped with mail shirts, formed of interlinked iron rings, which reached below the knee, and an iron cap with a nosepiece, they fought with spear, sword and the two-handed Danish axe. Quartered in garrisons at strategic points, they could be assembled quickly to form the nucleus around which the fyrd would gather. The professional corps of housecarls was paid and supported by a heavy land tax, the successor of the Danegeld which, like so many other English practices, had been adapted from one purpose to another, in this case from buying off the invading Danes to raising an army of defense. This war tax, assessed at two shillings a hide, had been instituted in 1016. It had been abolished in 1051 by King Edward as an economy move, but it was in force again at the time of his death, and it does not appear that these royal guards were ever disbanded. They died almost to a man at Hastings.

This standing professional force could be augmented in times of national or local need by calling up the militia or the fyrd, a word meaning any kind of land or sea force. All able-bodied men between the ages of sixteen and fifty were liable to serve, if required, in their own vicinity during the day without pay. If they were unable to return home by nightfall, they were paid. These local levies, ill-disciplined and ill-equipped as they were, were ideally suited for speedy mobilization to repel border raids and Danish incursions, but they could prove a hindrance in a major battle, as Hastings demonstrated. Above this mass levy stood a far more select militia, the freemen who owed service for their land. They were recruited by a system of considerable sophistication, which required that each provide the service of a particular man, a warrior trained and equipped to fight, or for an equivalent substitute. Each five-hide unit of land (a hide could vary from 40 to 120 acres depending upon its locality) was required to supply one warrior, a man specially designated, whose subsistence and pay were provided by the land unit, as is shown by an entry in the Berkshire section of Domesday Book (D.B.I. 56B):

> If the King sent an army anywhere, only one soldier went from five hides, and four shillings were given him from each hide as subsistence and wages for two months. This money, indeed, was not sent to the King but was given to the soldiers. If anyone summoned on an expedition did not go, he forfeited his land to the King. But if anyone for the sake of remaining behind promised to send another in his place, and yet he who was to have been sent remained behind, his lord was freed of obligation by the payment of fifty shillings.

This part-time warrior rendered for his unit the national service required in respect to fortress work, bridge-building and fighting, leaving his untrained neighbors to provide the one shilling a day required for his service, which was limited to a period of sixty days. He could be called up again and again, the only limitation being the need to provision him for further periods of sixty days.

This method of recruitment was far more efficient than was the Continental feudal system, in which tenants were required to perform forty days of unpaid service a year. Armed and trained men could be quickly mobilized to serve on land or at sea, as long as their provisions lasted. Not infrequently the army that could remain in the field the longest emerged as the victor.

These part-time soldiers and sailors may have numbered ten thousand men, one-fifth of the freemen-landowners of military age, out of the total population of approximately one and a half million. They could be called up, in theory, only by the King, and they assembled and fought grouped according to their shires, under the banner of their local lord. These warrior-representatives were spread over all England, each churl, thegn and lesser earl being the liege man of one of the five great earls: Harold, his two brothers Gyrth and Leofwine, Edwin of Mercia, and Morcar of Northumbria.

It appears that these "fyrdworthy" men, as they were designated, could be required to serve on land or sea but not on both, whereas the housecarls were both soldiers and sailors. Similarly, the taxation system provided for the provision of ships by coastal towns, which were excused from land-tax assessment. The English navy was partly professional, composed of royal ships manned by paid crews, and partly selective; the ships and crews drawn from certain ports, particularly the five major ports of southeast England, and by territorial obligation. The navy was originated by King Alfred, who built bigger and longer ships than did the Danes, and subsequent kings kept the fleet in existence until 1049, when King Edward disbanded some of the royal ships, reducing the standing fleet to five vessels. *The Anglo-Saxon Chronicle* relates that in 1066 Harold was able to collect an exceptionally large sea fyrd. From the scanty information available it is possible to conclude that after 1051 the fleet ceased to be solely professional, and greater reliance was placed on the recruitment of ships and crews from individual ports, whose warrior-crewmen were paid at the rate of three and a half pennies per day. Nonetheless, ships and crews continued to be provided by the greater earls and important prelates, for we read that the Bishop of

Worcester paid a man who was both the commander of his land levies and the master of his ship. Each three hundred hides of land was required to provide one ship, manned by sixty armed oarsmen. The ports of Dover, Sandwich, Hythe, Romney and Hastings supplied twenty ships apiece, each manned by a steersman and twenty-one crewmen, for fifteen days annually.

The ships available for speedy mobilization were probably constructed on the principle of the Norse longship of which the Gokstadt ship, unearthed in 1880, provides a typical example. It measured 72 feet in length and it was 15 feet 6 inches wide amid ship and 6 feet from keel to bulwark. It was propelled by 16 oars and one square sail. Sizes varied, and some of the longships were rowed by 64 oars and carried 140 men. Sea warfare was conducted at close quarters, by hand-to-hand fighting.

The navy of England was famed throughout Europe. In 1047 King Sweyn of Denmark requested King Edward to send fifty ships to help him in his war against Norway, and two years later Emperor Henry III asked the English king to blockade Flanders and to prevent his vassal, Count Baldwin, from escaping by sea. Edward refused the first request, but in 1049 the English fleet cruised in the Channel until Baldwin capitulated. These references prove that the capability of the English fleet was well-known abroad.

Harold thus inherited a powerful army and an efficient fleet, both of which he had commanded for fourteen years. At his call stood three thousand professional soldiers, fierce Saxons and Danes, famed fighting men equipped with armor and weapons as modern as those of the Norman knights, trained to act together and experienced in fighting under his leadership. To augment this standing army he could call upon ten thousand trained part-time warriors. To support this efficient force, he could put into the field in each locality a mass of peasants, armed with clubs and sticks, who, because of their knowledge of the vicinity, could act as scouts and guides. Around the coasts lay hundreds of ships, manned by men experienced in seamanship, ready to sail at short notice. The Channel ports could muster one hundred ships, a fleet that could be doubled or trebled by the arrival of the vessels sent by the big towns and the great landowners.

Harold, as he assessed his armed forces, could justifiably feel confident that he could repel any invader sufficiently foolhardy to attempt the conquest of England. At a meeting of the Witan at Westminster at Easter, which fell between 16 and 23 April, the King outlined his plans for the defense of England. As was the custom, he "wore his crown" at a state ceremony, and he took the opportunity to make certain ecclesiastical appointments. He filled the vacancy at the Abbey of Abingdon caused by the death of Abbot Odric, and he took from Stigand the Abbey of Ely, which the latter held simultaneously with his archbishopric contrary to ecclesiastical law, and gave it to a monk named Thurstan. But Stigand was allowed to keep a large share of the abbey's lands.

The peaceful Easter festival had barely ended when there came an omen of doom, such as no man had ever seen before, states *The Anglo-Saxon Chronicle*. On the night of 24 April the heavens blazed with a fearful light as a hairy star passed across the southern sky. For seven nights and more, from sunset to dawn, its bright orb and fiery rays set the sky ablaze. In every land men gazed and wondered. The comet, declared the vulgar, was sent to kindle a fire upon earth. No such token appeared without a reason. Chroniclers in France, Germany, Poland and Italy remarked the comet's appearance, each and all linking it with the coming struggle for England's crown. The learned expounded the omen. Holy men, prophets of evil, forecast the woes to come. In his cell at Malmesbury, an aged monk named Aethelmar, a dabbler in the arts and sciences, broke forth into a flood of terrible prediction: The star had come to bring woes to many mothers; he had seen the same sign in former days; now it had come to bring a far more fearful disaster upon his native land. Such another sign had ushered in the troubles in the reign of the martyred Edward; famines, earthquakes and civil commotion had followed hard upon the track of the blazing star. Only a few years later (989) the same comet had heralded the renewal of the great Scandinavian invasions and the ravaging of England. Another such awful warning had closed the year of the horrors of the war between Edmund Ironside and Canute (1017). It had shone over the grave of the English hero, a beacon lighting the path of the Danish conqueror. So now, foretold the aged monk, some great event was portended; some great ruler would soon meet his doom, but who could say whether the mighty sword which hung over the world was drawn on behalf of Harold or William? From that day no man doubted that the sword of the Lord was drawn; it would not be returned to its scabbard until it had drunk its fill.

The appearance of Halley's Comet in 1066, between 2 April and 30 May (*Notices of the Royal Astronomical Society,* Vol. 10, p. 51), as it had done in 989, struck terror into the hearts of Englishmen. The Bayeux Tapestry vividly depicts King Harold seated upon his throne, with a servant drawing his attention to the sign in the sky. As superstitious as his subjects, Harold must have wondered when the blow would fall.

Six

The Diversion

Tostig struck first. He had fled to Flanders in October 1065, consumed with hatred for his brother Harold, who had failed to support him when his Northumbrian subjects revolted. Now, at the crucial moment of their fate, the two eldest surviving sons of Godwine were divided.

When Tostig heard of Harold's coronation, he schemed how he might exploit the situation to his own advantage. His first move, it seems, was to offer his services to his relative by marriage, William. He was soon at Rouen, urging the invasion of England, promising his help and the support of his friends in the North. William accorded him a brotherly welcome and listened to what he had to say. He doubted, probably, whether the exiled Earl could be of much use to him, until Tostig asked permission to raise volunteers and recruit ships for a raid on the English coast. The subtle mind of William saw an advantage to be gained. Tostig might prove a useful diversion. He allowed him to sail, hoping that his appearance on the coast would frighten Harold into mobilizing his forces too soon. The English fyrd, William knew, would disband after sixty days in the field.

Tostig sailed in May, landing on and harrying the Isle of Wight, where he collected provisions before he was driven away by the vigilant English fleet. Prevented by contrary winds from returning to Normandy, he went to Sandwich, where he enlisted supporters, sailing up the east coast with sixty ships. He entered the Humber and ravaged the coasts of his old earldom until he was driven off by Earl Edwin. Many of his supporters deserted him, and he sailed with twelve ships to Scotland, taking refuge with his blood brother Malcolm. Tostig's next moves are uncertain, and for a description of them we rely solely on Norwegian sagas, which relate that he went first to Flanders and then to Denmark, where he sought the help of his cousin King Sweyn, would could offer nothing better than a Danish earldom. He sailed next, so the story goes, to Norway, where he found Hardrada considering the invasion of England. Tostig asked for assistance in recovering his earldom, but the Norwegian King was doubtful of the success of such a hazardous enterprise.

The English housecarls were so brave that one of them was better than any two Northmen (a remarkable tribute to Harold's despised soldiers), said Hardrada.

Astutely, Tostig offered the one argument that might influence the Norwegian. Hardrada had failed to conquer Denmark because of lack of support within that kingdom. In northern England, Tostig urged, he would find ready supporters, men of Scandinavian race who were anxious to overthrow Saxon rule. Tostig's own friends would rise to Hardrada's support. With their help, Hardrada could conquer England and set her Imperial Diadem on his head. Tostig would become his man and serve him faithfully as under-king.

Tostig's arguments, the sagas state, convinced Hardrada. He ordered the levy of half the fighting men of his kingdom and the collection of two hundred longships to carry them to England. Tostig was sent in advance with seventeen ships to the Orkneys, Norwegian possessions, to recruit men and ships.

Tostig's moves had the result William hoped. His raids on the English coasts made Harold think that the invasion was imminent. Early in June, he ordered the mobilization of the southern fyrd, which was instructed to assemble in Sussex, at the place of the Hoar Apple Tree, a noted landmark on a spur of the South Downs, seven miles behind Hastings. The fleet was sent to patrol the Channel, and Harold moved to the Isle of Wight. The English mobilization was completed by 8 July.

Seven

The Wind

William's spies informed him of Harold's mobilization. There was considerable trade between the English and Norman ports, and a messenger would have experienced no difficulty in reaching Normandy. Travellers' tales and the gossip of ports probably told William of Hardrada's preparations and of Tostig's plans.

Like all Europe, William watched the comet flaming in the sky. The least superstitious of men, he shrugged off the omen, but he did not discourage talk of its portentous significance. "A great kingdom is about to change its king," whispered the vulgar; William thought so too. The stars in their courses might be fighting for him, but he had more practical things to consider, the thousand and one details that could ensure the success of the enterprise against England. Failure to attend to them could bring disaster.

William's imagination leaped ahead. Certain problems solved themselves. The mobilization of fighting men was not his direct concern. In the feudal host, the great barons rode to war, each followed by a train of knights, armed and ready to fight. The volunteers and mercenaries flocking to Normandy provided their own equipment. The ships and crews required to ferry the army across the Channel were supplied by the great barons and prelates. William needed only to train his international force to act together and to feed it as it assembled and while it waited to embark. In England, it could live off the land for several weeks.

The time in which the army could survive across the sea was strictly limited. Therein lay William's greatest difficulty. He had to bring King Harold to battle at once. If Harold stood off and refused to fight a decisive battle or, worse still, laid waste the countryside, denying the Normans food, the great adventure could end in ignominious failure, possibly in disaster.

Duke William assessed the risks he faced. He possessed an acute and reasoning mind. He was capable of thinking out the logical consequences of his decisions. His career shows him to have been a realist, a man who calculated and planned carefully. He had committed himself to the invasion of England, a hazardous enterprise that was too far advanced for him to withdraw. His plan was based on a slender thread. He gambled that the impetuous Harold would give battle at once, near the coast. At all costs William had to avoid being drawn into the interior to fight on ground of Harold's choosing, where and when it suited him.

First, he had to ferry his army across the Channel. England, William knew, possessed a powerful fleet, manned by experienced seamen, the best in Europe. The Norman ships, heavily laden transports hurriedly built and crewed by men who had no experience of sea warfare, would be easy prey for the English warships, if they were caught at sea. The great invasion fleet could be destroyed before it reached the shore. The Normans had to give the English fleet the slip, to cross the Channel where and when they were unexpected. But such a maneuver would still not solve the entire difficulty, for the English Channel fleet could still cut off the Norman retreat and block supplies and reinforcements.

William planned to land about ten thousand men on the shores of England. Harold, he knew, could mobilize an army far more numerous and partly professional. The English housecarls were as well-trained and equipped as were the Continental knights. They were famed throughout Europe. The Saxons and Danes of the fyrd were fierce warriors, large, powerful men who could be mustered quickly. William's caution, following his landing in England, shows that he had a deep respect for England's army.

William planned to overcome the first danger by crossing the Channel quickly and by night. The English Channel fleet could not remain at sea indefinitely, and he thought he could avoid it by a sudden, unexpected crossing. Once his army had landed, he believed, Harold would rush to fight at once. William would lure him to the coast and defeat him by means of his horsed knights, the resource Harold would think it impossible for the Normans to transport across the sea. William planned to land three thousand men with their horses on the shores of England. With them as the spearhead of the army, he would achieve victory and win England's crown.

By early July, William knew that England's army, the professional housecarls and the fyrds of the southern counties, was assembled in Sussex waiting for him. The English army would remain an effective force as long as its provisions lasted, for two months at most. William faced the same difficulty; his volunteer and mercenary soldiers and the crews of his ships could be kept together only as long as they were fed and paid. If he delayed crossing the Channel until after 8 September, the English army might disband, but so might his own, and by then the summer would be over and the tempestuous autumn far advanced. In the outcome, William's dilemma was decided for him by the unpredictable weather of the English Channel. In all history, seldom can the weather have played such a decisive part.

William pondered his problems. According to Wace, "he got together carpenters, smiths and other workmen, so that great stir was seen at all the ports of Normandy, in the collection of wood and materials, cutting of planks, framing of ships and boats, stretching sails and rearing masts, with great pain and at great cost. They spent all one summer and autumn in fitting up the fleet and collecting the forces; and there was no knight in the land, no good sergeant archer, nor peasant of stout heart, and of age for battle, that the duke did not summon to go with him to England, promising rents to the soldiers and honors to the barons." The fame of the Duke went forth through many lands, in tales of how he meant to cross the sea against Harold. Soldiers came flocking to him, one by one, two by two, four by four; by fives and sixes, sevens and eights, nines and tens. He retained them all, giving them much and promising more. Many came by agreement made beforehand; many bargained for land in England; some required pay, allowances and gifts, and the Duke was often obliged to give at once to those who could not wait for the result. William made two stipulations: The soldiers had to be "tall and stout," and the commanders and standard-bearers had to be reputable for wisdom and age, so that "each of them might be taken for a prince rather than a leader." Into the duchy poured the volunteers and mercenaries. A contingent of Norman knights rode from Sicily. They may have provided the answer to William's greatest problem.

Historians glibly state that William brought his mounted knights to England. At the Battle of Hastings some three thousand Norman, French, Flemish and Breton knights fought, each seated astride a trained war-horse. No one seems to have stopped to consider how that number of horses, fragile, nervous animals, was loaded, carried across the sea in open boats, and unloaded at Pevensey, where, for all William knew, Harold's army might have been drawn up to contest his landing. William overcame the difficulty of horse transport, as the Bayeux Tapestry depicts, but its vivid pictures give only the merest hint of how he did it.

The problem of transporting horses by sea must have vexed William early in the pre-invasion period. He may have considered the feat impossible, but for the Normans to fight on foot was unthinkable; somehow he had to carry three thousand horses to England. Neither the Normans nor any other people in Northern Europe had any experience at getting horses into ships and out again on such a scale. But the Romans had done it, the Duke's priestly advisers may have told him. Lanfranc, we know, was well-versed in classical literature; he and other priests may have read Julius Caesar's *War Commentaries* and the works of the later Roman historians, who described the great invasion by Aulius Platius in A.D. 48. Caesar, they could have told William, on his second raid in 54 B.C., landed two thousand cavalry near Deal in southern England from 288 specially built transport vessels, which had sailed from Boulogne with the fleet of 800 ships on the night of 6 July. But to William's question of how the Romans loaded and unloaded their horses, they could only have returned a shake of the head, for Caesar does not explain.

By the twelfth and thirteenth centuries, the transport of horses was commonplace in military technology, but by then ships were larger, deeper and wider. During the reigns of the English Kings John and

Henry III, horses were loaded and unloaded through doors cut in the ship's side, like a "bung-hole in a barrel," as the chronicler Joinville describes, and the horses were secured during the voyage in temporary stalls constructed from hurdles. An elephant was brought to England during Henry's reign. Norman experience in horse transport by sea has been discussed by Mr. D. P. Waley in "Combined Operations In Sicily, A.D. 1060–81," *Papers of the British School at Rome,* Vol. XXII (New Series, Vol. IX), 1954.

The Norsemen, it should be explained, had established themselves in southern Italy early in the tenth century. In the eleventh century their numbers were increased by the arrival of malcontents and exiles from Normandy, who founded a kingdom at Naples and a dukedom at Apulia. In the year 1038 several hundred Norman knights were shipped across the Strait of Messina to assist in the Byzantine attempt to reconquer Sicily from the Saracens, an unsuccessful campaign in which Harald Hardrada, as we have seen, held a command. In 1060 the Normans invaded Sicily on their own.

The Christian conquest of Sardinia, Sicily and Malta was, remarks Waley, both a rehearsal and an essential preliminary for the Crusades. The tactics employed by the Normans in their conquest of southern Italy and Sicily demonstrate their naval technique and show the Vikings finding their sea legs again after many decades as farmers and cavalrymen in Normandy. Waley deals with the operations extending from the first raid on the port of Messina from the Calabrian mainland in 1060 to the abandonment of the siege of Naples in 1078. The Norman army, he observes, was in essence a cavalry force; it transported its horses from the mainland to Sicily and fought upon them. While admitting the possibility that the Normans owed their mastery of this technological advance to their own ingenuity, Waley thinks it more probable that they acquired it from the Byzantines, who were accustomed to the transport of horses, which they had carried since 961 in ships specially designed for the purpose, in which ramps could be let down from the side, making it possible for the cavalry to ride into action when the ships beached. The Normans in Sicily had an opportunity to learn this technique as early as 1038, but there are no references to their use of it in the eleventh century, and Mr. Waley concludes that they did not transport war-horses in such specially constructed vessels, which were probably held in a central pool at Constantinople. The Normans, he thinks, employed the ships they found in the ports they had overrun, war galleys and fishing and trading vessels capable of being adapted for naval use. It is unlikely that the Normans built their own ships before 1076; no single source suggests that they did, and one implies that they set out to capture the port of Bari in order to find ships with which to undertake the siege of Palermo. The warships they found in Italian ports were probably galleys—long, open ships similar to the Norse longship, rather than the more rounded and larger dromon, the Byzantine ship of the line.

How, then, did the Normans in Italy load and unload their horses? G. Malaterra (*De Rebus Gestis Rogerii Calabriae et Sicilae Comitis,* ed. E. Pontieri in *Rerum Italicarium Scriptores,* n.s., I, 58) describes how, near Otranto in 1061, the Norman knights dug out a ramp in the cliff shore and led their horses aboard. We do not know if they had adopted that method previously, and it seems possible that they abandoned it after the year 1081, when they first built special ships for overseas landings. The ramp method of loading left unsolved the problem of unloading, possibly on a hostile shore.

Prior to 1066, the Normans in Italy had engaged in four campaigns that had required combined operations. They had made three landings in the years 1060–1061 in the neighborhood of Messina, and on the third attempt they had captured the city. The ships they used are described as "galleys." According to the figures given by Aimé of Monte Cassino (*Storia dei Normanni,* ed. V. de Bartholomaas in *Fonti per la Storia d'Italia,* pp. 248–55) for the Messina landing in 1061, thirteen ships carried 270 chevaliers with their horses and returned to the Calabrian shore for 170 more. When further reinforced, the Norman cavalry totalled one thousand. From these figures, Waley estimates that the ships carried an average maximum of twenty cavalrymen with their horses. Ten years later, at the siege of Palermo, fifty or sixty ships were used.

The first landing in 1060 was a reconnaissance only. Sixty Norman knights landed at the port of Messina, which was some distance from the city, achieved surprise and drew out some members of the Moslem garrison, whom they defeated by means of a feigned flight. They then withdrew, taking with them the horses they had captured. The Normans must have considered the operation successful, for, in the spring of 1061, 160 knights crossed the strait. They looted two towns and returned to their vessels, which they had left at Faro at the extreme northeastern point of Sicily. They found the sea was too rough to embark, which implies that it was too rough to load and convey horses, and they had to wait for three days before recrossing the strait. They made a third crossing, in the same year, landing two hundred horsemen four and one-half miles south of Messina. They ran into a Moslem party, whom they routed, capturing a large treasure. Meanwhile the ships returned across the strait, bearing reinforcements, which brought the Norman strength to 450 horsemen, who had no difficulty in capturing Messina. Further reinforcements brought the Norman strength to about one thousand horsemen and the same number of infantry.

The efficiency of the Normans in unloading their cavalry was never fully tested, points out Waley, for the Moslems did not, on any of the three occasions, attempt to defend the coastline, and they were taken by surprise. Five years after the Sicilian landings, William of Normandy landed a large cavalry army on the coast of England, and among his cosmopolitan force were knights from southern Italy. As they were probably the only members of his force who had experience in transporting cavalry across the sea, William would doubtless probably have consulted them. "History sometimes does come rather near to repeating itself," says Waley, and he remarks, "It is possible that lessons in combined operations learned on the shores of Sicily in 1060–61 were applied between Normandy and England in 1066, just as those learned on the southern Sicilian coast in 1943 were applied—this time between England and Normandy—to the landings of 1944."

Waley's researches prove that the Normans in Italy were experienced in horse transport across the sea; there can be little argument that William drew on their experience. What advice did the Norman contingent from southern Italy give him? We know only that on 27 September the Normans loaded about four hundred ships with horses, in addition to their riders, and that next morning they disembarked at Pevensey. How William may have accomplished this feat must be left to later consideration. For the moment we can leave the practical Duke considering the problem. He had many pressing matters to deal with.

William called his barons to counsel with him. He met them at Bonneville-sur-Touques on 15 June and again on the 18th at Caen, where a great concourse of nobles and prelates had gathered for the dedication of the Minster of Holy Trinity, one of the two great expiatory foundations promised by the Duke and Duchess for their marital sin. The other was the Abbey of St. Stephen, built at Caen, of which Lanfranc had been appointed abbot in 1063. William and Matilda lavished gifts on both foundations, and they gave to God the first fruit of their bodies, their daughter Cecily, who became in time the renowned abbess of her mother's foundation.

The Duke concerned himself with a number of ecclesiastical matters. The Church in Normandy, it seems, took a cautious view of William's expedition, from which he might never return. The Abbot of Marmoutier sent a monk to ask for confirmation of recent gifts by the Duke's son Robert, and he was asked also to ratify the rights of the See of Avranches to dispose of certain properties, "when Duke William was setting out across the sea." Many of the barons who were preparing to go overseas also confirmed the gifts they had made to religious foundations. The Church stood to gain by the success of the venture; William confirmed the grant of land at Steyning in England to the Abbey of Fécamp, the gift to take effect "if God should give him victory." With the Church well bribed to support his family in his absence or in the event of his death, William provided for the administration of the duchy while he was overseas, or if he failed to return. He assembled the chief barons and extracted from them a solemn oath of fealty to his fourteen-year-old son Robert, and he appointed Duchess Matilda to act as regent. Knowing from his own experience how inadequate such an oath could be and foreseeing the dangers of minority reign, he chose three prominent nobles, Roger de Beaumont, Roger de Montgomery,* and Hugh, the son of Richard, the Viscount of Avranches, to assist in the administration.

About that time another stroke of fortune befell William. Count Conan of Brittany died. William certainly gained by the death of his recently rebellious vassal, for it secured his western border during his absence, and it has been suggested that he poisoned Conan.

Historians, however, consider the allegation that William was a

* Ordericus Vitalis says he stayed in Normandy: Wace records his presence, or perhaps his son's, at Hastings.

secret poisoner unlikely. It is certainly remarkable that it is a Norman writer only (Will-Gem VII, 33) who relates the story. According to this late and dubious authority, Conan, when he heard that William was preparing the invasion of England, sent to wish him good luck in his enterprise and at the same time to demand the cession of Normandy to himself, as the lawful heir. If William did not at once surrender the duchy, he would assert his rights with his whole army. William, we are told, was somewhat frightened, but God delivered him from his danger. The messenger, a Breton noble, undertook to rid him of Conan who was besieging the fortress of Château-Contier in Anjou. He anointed the Count's gloves, bridle and hunting horn with poison. In the act of making his triumphal entry into the town, Conan put on the gloves, grasped the bridle and unwittingly raised his hands to his mouth. Before long he was dead. The truth seems to be that Conan died suddenly, and, as his death was convenient to William, the latter was believed to be his rival's murderer.

With his rear protected, William concentrated on war. He needed to create a disciplined force out of the miscellaneous contingents that were gathering to make up the invasion army. The great vassals were assembling with their knights, and volunteers and mercenaries were pouring in from Maine, Brittany, Picardy, Flanders, Anjou, Burgundy and Poitou. Many were mere brigands, adventurers seeking plunder; others were filled with the crusading spirit. One, at least, sought revenge. Eustace, Count of Boulogne, had an old score to settle with the insolent citizens of Dover, with whom he had crossed swords on a visit to England in 1051.

The strength of William's international, French-speaking army is variously stated by contemporary authorities. The most reasonable estimate places it at about 7,500 fighting men, a figure deduced partly from the size and number of ships that assembled at the mouth of the River Dive, near modern Deauville, early in August. According to the quotas allotted to, or promised by, the nobles and prelates of Normandy and compiled by Ordericus Vitalis, there were 782 ships. Wace, on the other hand, who says that he was told the number by his father, gives the figure at 696. William of Jumièges says that the vessels numbered 3,000. The truth is probably that there were about 700 ships of various types and sizes, and innumerable small craft. Ships of the type that the

Normans were likely to have built, it has been estimated, could have carried about twenty men each; but there were more than men to be conveyed: stores, barrels of wine, sheaves of arrows, bundles of lances and, of course, horses.

It was William's problem to weld this heterogeneous force into an army. We may assume legitimately that during the assembly period he exercised his knights, training them to act together, not a difficult undertaking, for, from wherever they came, they used the same weapons and fought in the same way. His great difficulty lay not in teaching them to fight, but in keeping them together, the great problem of medieval warfare. Seven thousand men had to be fed, paid and housed, for if abundant food had not been supplied, they would have devastated the countryside. For a whole month, states William of Poitiers, the Duke "utterly forbade pillage," and "he made generous provision both for his own knights and for those from other parts, but he did not allow any of them to take their sustenance by force. The flocks and herds of the peasantry pastured unharmed throughout the province. The crops waited undisturbed for the sickle without either being trampled by the knights in their pride, or ravaged out of greed by plunderers. A weak and unarmed man might watch the swarm of soldiers without fear, and following his horse singing as he would."

Early in August William went to the mouth of the Dive, where the fleet was assembled. His embassy returned from Rome, bringing the Pope's blessing for his enterprise and bearing gifts, a consecrated banner and a precious ring containing, it was alleged, a hair from the head of St. Peter. The Holy Father had given judgment for him. The crown of England was his by right, the Church had declared. William had achieved a great diplomatic victory.

About that time, according to the chronicler William of Poitiers (and it seems quite likely true), Harold sent spies across the Channel. One of them was captured, and, though he tried to conceal his errand, the Duke saw through his disguise. "It was not necessary," he told the man, "for Harold to throw away his gold and silver in buying the fidelity and fraud of men like you who come clandestinely among us to ferret out our plans." The King of England, he said, would know his designs quicker than he expected. He would have more certain knowledge of them when he saw the Duke of Normandy in person. He ordered the man, "Tell him that if he does not see me within one year in the place where he now strives to make safe against my coming, he may rest quiet for the rest of his days and need fear no harm from me."

The Norman magnates who heard it were appalled at this rash speech. Some of them, probably the same men who had earlier expressed their fears at Lillebonne, in the words of William of Poitiers, "exaggerated the resources of Harold and minimized their own." The Duke sought to restore their confidence. Wars are not won by numbers but by courage, he reminded the doleful. Harold, he told them, fought to retain what he had wrongfully seized. The Normans fought for lawful claim. "Strong in this knowledge, we shall overcome the dangers and win a happy victory, great honors and high renown," he exhorted them.

By 12 August, the fleet was ready to embark the army of invasion. William ordered a clerk to write down the names of the principal men of the army and he and they attended mass in the church at Dives, a solid Norman building that stands to this day. On the west wall, in 1869, were inscribed the names of the "Conqueror's Companions," drawn up by a committee of French scholars.

The invasion fleet awaited only William's command to embark stores, men and horses, to man the oars, set the sails and move out of the estuary into the Channel. Whether or not William intended to invade England while Harold's army stood ready to meet him, or to wait until after 8 September, when the sixty day period of the fyrd's service would expire, the weather decided matters for him. A series of deep depressions developed over northern France and southern England, producing strong, gale-force winds, probably accompanied by storms of lashing rain.

For nearly a month the army kicked its heels in idleness, awaiting a change of wind to the south. Many knights began to despair. The common soldiers muttered that "the man must be mad who wished to subjugate a foreign country" and that "God opposed him and withheld the (right) wind." They reminded each other that, when William's father had proposed a similar attempt on England, he had in like manner been frustrated. The attempt of Robert II to invade England in 1034 had come to naught when his fleet was driven ashore and wrecked on the Island of Jersey. It was the fate of the ducal family to aspire to things beyond its reach and to find God its adversary, muttered the malcontents.

Suddenly, on 8 September, the weather improved and the winds calmed, but they still blew from the west, which impeded Channel crossing by square-rigged sailing ships. William seized the opportunity to move his army farther up the coast, to St. Valéry in the Somme estuary, where the fleet would be nearer to the English coast, leaving only a sixty mile sea crossing. This transfer from the Dive was effected, but at considerable cost. A number of ships were lost, sailors and soldiers were drowned, and others broke faith with the Duke and made off in craven flight. William prudently caused the bodies of those who had perished to be buried secretly, and he concealed the loss of vital supplies by increasing the daily ration. He exhorted the fearful and put courage into the despondent. He succeeded in keeping his army together.

On the same day, 8 September, Harold's army disbanded. Food ran out, and members of the fyrd began to return to their homes. The fleet, many ships of which had been damaged in the great storm, was sent to London, toward which Harold marched with his housecarls. The coast of Sussex lay open to invasion.

Eight

The Dilemma

The wind that delayed William blew Harald Hardrada southward. He had sailed some weeks before from Sogne Fjord near Bergen, with two hundred longships and forty smaller vessels, which, if the bigger ships had the capacity of the Gokstadt ship (32 rowers and a similar number of reserves), could have carried as many as eighteen thousand men. It was the greatest and the last Norse expedition of conquest. It was almost a migration. Hardrada took with him half the able-bodied men of Norway, and his queen, Elizabeth, her two daughters and his son Olaf, as well as his great ingot of gold, his loot from Byzantium, which required the combined strength of twelve youths to carry. Before he sailed, he nominated Magnus, his son by his second "wife" Thora, as subking to rule in his absence and to act as his viceroy when he became, after the conquest of England, Emperor of the North. With the wind at his stern, Hardrada sailed to Shetland and the Orkney Islands, which were Scandinavian earldoms, to recruit allies.

The fleet left Norway under the shadow of doom. Terrible portents and fearful omens plagued the Vikings, according to the sagas, whose poets may have benefited from after knowledge. While the fleet lay at the Solund Islands, at the mouth of Sogne Fjord, a man named Gyrd on the King's ship had a dream. He dreamed he saw a great witch standing on the island, with a fork in one hand and a trough in the other. He also saw over all the fleet, and saw that a fowl was sitting upon every ship's stern, and that these fowls were all ravens or ernes. And the witch sang this song:

> From the east I'll 'tice the king,
> To the west the king I'll bring;
> Many a noble bone will be
> In battle left for me.
> Ravens o'er Giuke's* ship are flitting,
> Eyeing the prey they think most fitting.
> Upon the stem I'll sail with them!
> Upon the stem I'll sail with them!

There was also a man called Thord, in a ship that lay not far from the King's ship. He dreamed one night that he saw King Harald's fleet coming to land, and he knew the land to be England. He saw a great battle array on the land, and he saw both sides begin to fight, with many banners flapping in the air. And before the army of the people of the country was riding a huge witch upon a wolf; and the wolf had a man's carcass in his mouth, and the blood was dripping from his jaws; and when he had eaten up one body she threw another into his mouth, and so one after another, and he swallowed them all. And she sang:

> Skade's eagle eyes
> The king's ill luck espies;
> Though glancing shields
> Hide the green fields,
> The king's ill luck she spies.
> To bode the doom of this great king,
> The flesh of bleeding men I fling
> To hairy jaw and hungry maw!
> To hairy jaw and hungry maw!

King Harald also dreamed one night that he was in Nidaros and that he met his brother King Olaf, who sang to him these verses:

> In many a fight
> My name was bright;
> Men weep, and tell
> How Olaf fell.

* Giuke was a celebrated Viking.

Thy death is near;
Thy corpse, I fear,
The crow will feed,
The witch-wife's steed.

Many other dreams and forebodings were told, and most of them were gloomy, according to the thirteenth-century compiler of the Norse sagas.

At Orkney, Hardrada was joined by earls Paul and Erlend, the two sons of Thorfin, who had died two years before after a reign of fifty years; by Godred, the Chief of Iceland, and by an unnamed Irish king, of Norwegian ancestry, no doubt. Hardrada left his wife and daughters in Orkney and sailed with his considerably enlarged fleet down the east coast of Scotland, where he was joined by Tostig, who brought his Flemish ships and a Scottish contingent provided by King Malcolm. The whole fleet, which numbered three hundred vessels, arrived off the mouth of the Tyne early in September. The combined host of northern Europe, commanded by its greatest warrior king, descended upon England near the day on which King Harold was forced to abandon his vigil on the south coast.

The two northern earls were taken unaware by Hardrada's invasion. No army barred his landing on the Yorkshire coast. For a week or more, the Norsemen ravaged and plundered the countryside. The district of Cleveland submitted without resistance, and Hardrada marched on Scarborough, whose citizens shut themselves within their walls. The Norseman's quick eye saw a way to overcome their defiance, without incurring the losses and delays of a long siege. The old town lay at the foot of a height, upon which the Norsemen raised a vast pile of wood, to which they set fire. They then hurled the burning timbers down upon the town; house after house caught fire, and the people surrendered. They were butchered to a man. A hurriedly assembled local fyrd was also put to the sword.

Laden with plunder, the Norsemen re-embarked on their ships and sailed south, entering the estuary of the Humber. They rowed up the river Ouse and cast anchor on its left bank, near the village of Riccall, nine miles from York, the capital of Northumbria, Morcar's earldom. Morcar and his brother Edwin assembled an army to meet the Norse invasion, news of which was carried to King Harold, now in London on his return from the south coast. The messenger probably took three days to cover the 190 miles from York, and Harold may have learned of Hardrada's invasion by 15 September.

The news placed him in a terrible dilemma. Force of circumstances had driven him from the south coast. The fyrd of the southern counties had disbanded. William might land at any moment. He could not cross the Channel while the wind was adverse, but it could swing to the south suddenly and unpredictably. William could embark his army, cross the Channel and land unopposed. On the other hand, he might not come. A thousand accidents could prevent him from sailing, and the wind might not change. The fierce equinoctial gales were due, and they could blow for weeks. The threat from William was still theoretical. The threat from Hardrada was real. Could Edwin and Morcar repel the Norse invasion?

Harold had known for months that England might be invaded simultaneously from north and south. The hosts of northern and westerr Europe were arrayed against him; the two greatest warriors of the ag thirsted for his crown. Harold believed he could defeat Hardrada anc William, if they came separately. If they landed at the same time, he planned to fight William himself and to leave Edwin and Morcar to deal with Hardrada. Now Hardrada had come with a huge fleet. Three hundred ships implied an enormous force of warriors. Harold had doubts about Edwin and Morcar. They were young and inexperienced, of doubtful loyalty, and the people of northern England were of Scandinavian descent. Almost within living memory Northumbria had been a Norse kingdom. The northerners might rise in support of a Norwegian king rather than rally to fight for a half-Saxon southerner. With Hardrada came Tostig, eager to regain his earldom, vengeful against the brother who had allowed his subjects to turn him out.

Little is known about Harold at this anxious time. Legend relates that he fell ill on his return to London and that he implored the help of the Holy Rood of Waltham Abbey, whose sworn votary he was. The abbot, Aethelsigne, spent a sleepless night in prayer, which was rewarded by the appearance of the deceased Edward, who bade him carry a message to the King. Tell Harold to be strong, he said, and of good courage, and to go forth to battle with the enemies of England. He himself by his prayers would guide and defend his people and would direct their righteous warfare to certain victory. The abbot sought Harold and told him of the message from his saintly predecessor. And Harold, recovered from his sickness and made hopeful by the cheering words of Edward, applied himself with redoubled zeal to the work that lay before him, according to the Anglo-Saxon chronicler.

Harold made up his mind. He decided to direct a knock-out blow against Hardrada. He rejected half-measures, any attempt to further divide his forces, which could result in his doing too little in one place and being too late in the other. A quick march, a speedy victory in the North, and he might yet be back in the South before William crossed the sea. Harold threw all his tremendous energy into the task. He mobilized his housecarls, who were strategically grouped in and around London, and he recalled the southern fyrd. All Saxon, Norman and Scandinavian chroniclers are unanimous in stating that Harold collected an immense army, the greatest force ever assembled by Anglo-Saxon England. Professor Freeman, the historian of the Norman Conquest, has culled references from many sources to show that Harold's army composed the whole force of southern England, an amazing tribute to the Anglo-Saxon system of recruitment, which enabled the fyrd to be reprovisioned and reassembled within two weeks or so of its disbandment.

Harold left London about 18 September, marching his army, which was arranged in seven divisions, up the old Roman road to York, enlisting en route the militia of the eastern counties, mobilized by his brothers Gyrth and Leofwine, and calling upon volunteers from such distant western shires as Worcester, as is shown by a reference in Domesday, which relates that an aged thegn joined the great march northward and gave his life for England. Harold's marshal, Bondig, led the march, and the chronicler of Abingdon records that the army rested neither day or night. Even at that pace York lay at least five days' march ahead.

Hardrada disembarked his army at Riccall. He left his fleet there with a detachment under the command of his son Olaf, to watch the English fleet which his spies told him had taken shelter near Tadcaster, up the River Wharfe, a tributary that entered the Ouse a mile above Riccall. With his base secured, Hardrada marched on York. During the two weeks that had elapsed since Hardrada's appearance off the Tyne,

Edwin and Morcar had assembled an army, composed it may be assumed, of the northern fyrd and their own retainers. Its numbers are beyond our estimation, but it was probably considerably weaker than the force of the southern counties, for Northumbria was by comparison sparsely populated, and the northern earls lacked the professional strength of the royal housecarls. Rather strangely, their army included many priests, for it is recorded that a hundred were killed in the great battle in which Edwin and Morcar sought to bar the Norsemen's advance on York.

The Englishmen of the North and the Norsemen met at Gate Fulford, then about two miles southeast of York, now a suburb of the city. The only account of the battle is that given in the *Sagas of the Norse Kings* (Samuel Laing translation) compiled by the Icelander Snorri Sturluson in the thirteenth century. He relied on ancient tradition, and he was ignorant of the geography of the area in which the battle was fought on Wednesday, 20 September. Nevertheless, the story told in the *Sagas* conforms to the traditional site of the battle. The road by which the Norsemen advanced toward York ran parallel to and some hundreds of yards from the north bank of the River Ouse. On the other side of the raised causeway lay a ditch and a fen, deep, broad and full of water. From the road the ground sloped gently to river and fen. The armies advanced to meet each other on ground on which neither of their flanks could be turned. These geographical features dictated a headlong clash, as Snorri describes.

Hardrada, who seems to have reached the spot first, drew up his men in line of battle, the strongest wing resting on the river, and the weakest extending to the ditch. He took his stand on the left, his giant frame and blond locks towering above friend and foe, beside him the banner of the Norsemen, the aptly named "Land-Ravager," the symbol of despoliation and massacre. The English launched their attack, Morcar gaining a quick advantage by throwing back the Norse right wing. Snorri tells the story:

> When King Harald saw that the English array had come to the ditch against him, he ordered the charge to be sounded, and urged on his men. He ordered the banner which was called the Land-ravager to be carried before him, and made so severe an assault that all had to give way before it; and there was a great loss among

> the men of the earls, and they soon broke into flight, some running up the river, some down, and the most leaping into the ditch, which was so filled with dead that the Norsemen could go dry-foot over the fen.

The broken English army fled, some to take refuge in York, others seeking their homes. Still others, Tostig's friends and relatives, as he had forecast, flocked to Hardrada's army, which must have suffered severely and was much strengthened by the new adherents. Hardrada advanced on York. When its citizens saw how the Norse King had gained so great a victory over so many chiefs, they were dismayed and doubted that they could make any opposition. They took counsel and sent a message to Hardrada offering to deliver up the city. On Sunday, 24 September, he proceeded to York and met outside the city an assembly of the people, who submitted to him, promising as hostages 150 children of the most considerable persons and, according to *The Chronicle of Abingdon,* recognizing him as king and agreeing to join him against King Harold. Anxious, no doubt, to gain the goodwill of his new subjects, Hardrada refrained from sacking the city, and in the evening he withdrew to Riccall, ordering a further assembly next day at Stamford Bridge, eight miles north of York, the meeting place of many roads, where he agreed to accept the hostages and to receive the surrender of Northumbria, to appoint officers, to bestow fiefs and to give out laws. That night at Riccall the Norsemen caroused. Their merriment drowned the tramp of the marching feet approaching York from the south.

King Harold reached Tadcaster on 24 September, the day York surrendered. He must have heard already of the disaster at Fulford. He marched the nine miles to York, entering the city that evening with the goodwill and consent of its citizens. He ordered that all the gates and walls be guarded, so that the Norsemen should receive no intelligence, and his army lay all night in the city.

The sun rose next day warm and strong, quickly dispelling the early-morning autumnal mists, a foretaste of impending heat. The Norsemen at Riccall were up early, preparing for their twelve-mile march across the countryside to a peaceful parley at Stamford Bridge. They felt so secure that most of them discarded their birnees, the iron-studded leather battle coats, storing them on the ships. Leaving behind a third of his force under the command of Prince Olaf, Hardrada marched to the meeting place, his men carrying only their shields, helmets, spears, swords and bows and arrows. When they reached the bridge at Stamford, the Norsemen spread out on both banks of the river Derwent. They were very merry. To the north rose the outline of the Yorkshire Wolds. The road to the south, from York, was obscured by a slight rise in the ground at Gate Helmsley, a village situated about a mile from Stamford.

It must have been about nine o'clock when the Norsemen, probably those scattered on the west of the river, noticed a cloud of dust billowing up the rise on the road from York. It lengthened and swelled as it advanced, and beneath it they discerned shining shields and bright armor. The nearer the army came, the greater it appeared, and to their northern imaginations the shining arms were like glancing ice. No one knew what army it could be. Hardrada called to Tostig to inquire. It might be hostile, but it could possibly be some of his friends coming to surrender and to seek mercy, answered the former Earl of Northumbria. The Norsemen's eyes strained for some sign by which the oncoming soldiers might be identified.

King Harold left York shortly after 6 A.M., slowing his men's march to allow the Norsemen to reach Stamford Bridge. Riding at the head of his army, Harold mounted the rise at Helmsley. Beneath him extended a low plain, through which meandered the Derwent, a reedy, sluggish stream twenty yards wide, bordered by alluvial flats and straddled by Stamford, which occupied slightly rising ground, and centered around the bridge across the river. The host of Norsemen stood spread out on both banks of the river, watching in astonishment the unexpected appearance of an immense army of horsemen and footmen. Harold ordered immediate attack.

The great battle fought on Monday, 25 September, at Stamford Bridge, is described only by the Icelander Snorri. Except for one dramatic detail of which he apparently did not hear, he drew on the ancient traditions of his race, which he collected two hundred years afterward. According to Snorri, the English fought on horseback and used archers, fighting in exactly the same way as did the Normans at Hastings, where the English adopted the tactic of static defense behind their shield wall. If Snorri is correct, the English were accustomed to fight on horseback and to use archers in conjunction with mounted men, and they changed their tactics at Hastings for special reasons.

How the English waged war in the eleventh century is the subject of considerable scholarly controversy. Many historians, led by Sir Charles Oman (*The Art of War in the Middle Ages,* 1924) deny that the English, prior to the Norman Conquest, fought on horseback, conceding only that they may have ridden to battle. Adherents of this school of thought declare that Snorri's story of the Battle of Stamford Bridge was derived, not from true tradition, but from an account of the Battle of Hastings, which he employed to tell the story of another battle, about which he knew nothing, or was colored by ideas of warfare current at the time when he wrote. In other words, Snorri is said to have invented his account of Stamford Bridge and to have improved it by relating incidents that occurred at Hastings. On the other hand, many modern historians accept Snorri's version as a true account, and they maintain that the English were as adept as were the Normans at combining horsemen and archers. In this interpretation the long-despised and decadent Anglo-Saxon army emerges as a force as up to date in its methods as the much-vaunted Normans. It was not the decayed, fossilized anachronism that its detractors claim. Both sides to the controversy produce evidence to support their case.

The English followed their usual method of waging war, employing the static shield-wall defense at Hastings, dismounting their troops, but not using archers, according to the first school. They forget, it is pointed out in rebuttal, that conditions at the Sussex battlefield were quite different from those in Yorkshire, which were ideal for cavalry tactics. Harold, maintains the second school, dismounted his housecarls at Hastings in order to strengthen his infantry-fyrd, and he lacked archers because he left them trailing behind on the road from York on his hurried dash to the south. The English fought on foot at Hastings because they always fought on foot, counter the old guard, who point to an incident recorded in the year 1055 to prove that the English were unaccustomed to fight on horseback and rejected it as a method of waging war.

The words of *The Anglo-Saxon Chronicle* can be taken to imply that in 1055 Earl Ralph of Hereford, a Norman, was beaten in a campaign against the Welsh "because he attempted to make the English fight on horseback contrary to their custom." The *Abingdon Chronicle,* on the other hand, is less definite, stating only, "But before there was any spear thrown, the English people fled because they were on horses." The first statement may be true, but it applies only to a particular campaign on the Welsh Marches; steep, broken, timbered country where the Herefordshire fyrd, long experienced in border warfare, may have preferred to fight on foot. Their earl's innovation was a failure. This episode applies only to a particular part of the English fyrd, the majority of whom were probably infantry.

This minor incident, and the failure of the English to fight on horseback at Hastings, forms the core of the argument that they never did so. A far stronger case is made for the modern assertion to the contrary. It is pointed out that during the Welsh campaign of 1063, Earl Tostig employed mounted men in the fighting on the plain bordering the north coast, on ground suitable for cavalry. When his predecessor, Earl Siward, invaded Scotland in 1054, he went, according to Florence of Worcester, *cum equestri exercitu.* King Macbeth's Norman allies, who were certainly mounted, were heavily defeated, and many were killed during the pursuit, which can hardly have happened if Earl Siward's men rode only to battle and dismounted to fight. In an even earlier reference, we find in *The Anglo-Saxon Chronicle* that during Edmund Ironside's pursuit of the Danes in Kent in 1016, "the army fled before him with their horses to Sheppey," the King slaying as many as he could overtake, which implies that his men were also mounted. Further proof is derived from a sketch drawn during the reign of Canute (reproduced in L. M. Larson's *Life of Canute,* 1912), which shows two horsemen, riding side by side, one throwing a spear and another a two-edged axe, the absence of hounds suggesting that the artist was not depicting a hunting scene. Harold himself, during the Norman campaign of 1064 against Brittany, served with credit with a Norman mounted force, and he was the companion-in-arms of the royal housecarls, who, several modern scholars claim, fought in the same way as the Norman knights. It is remarkable, also, that the authors of *The Anglo-Saxon Chronicle* should instinctively apply the Saxon word *cniht* to a mounted soldier, rather than employ the Norman term *chevaller.* Their use of the word, which became accepted as a term of Anglo-

Norman chivalry, does not suggest that a mounted soldier was a novelty in England in 1066.

Proof that the English used archers in battle is less easily discovered, as the Anglo-Saxon chroniclers used the same term for both lance and arrow, but it would have been strange if they had scorned such a well-established weapon, particularly as they became so adept with it after the Conquest. The English archers, like those of Normandy and France, were peasants who marched to battle on foot, and Harold's failure to employ them at Hastings, where their absence made a notable contribution to the Norman victory, can be accounted for by his hurried dash from the north, during which they were left struggling in the rear of his mounted housecarls.

These references suggest that Snorri's story of mounted Englishmen and archers at Stamford Bridge is not so improbable as was at one time thought. Nevertheless, his account of the battle carries the stigma of remarkable similarity to incidents described at Hastings and invites the charge that he portrayed the battle in terms of thirteenth-century warfare.

Snorri's description of English methods of attack by javelin-throwing horsemen, of their flight and pursuit by the Norsemen, who break their ranks to follow, and of the death of Hardrada, who fell mortally wounded by an arrow through his throat, is remarkably similar to descriptions of incidents at Hastings. Snorri's reliance on Hastings is confirmed, claimed his detractors, by his ignorance of local geography around York and his inaccuracies with respect to the family relationships of the English leaders. Snorri cannot be trusted, asserts Oman, because he says that Earl Morcar was King Harold's brother, that he fell at Fulford, and that Siward's son, Earl Waltheof, then a child, took part in the battle. R. W. Chambers (*England Before the Norman Conquest,* 1926), in rebuttal, concedes Snorri's inaccuracies but reasonably observes "these are points with regard to which the Norse invaders might well be in error," and he remarks that *The Anglo-Saxon Chronicle* makes similar mistakes about the Norse leaders. Such errors, he claims, do not invalidate the documents of any race.

Chambers finds Snorri and *The Anglo-Saxon Chronicle* in agreement on detail after detail in respect to the Battle of Fulford, the capture of York, and the events leading up to the Battle of Stamford

Bridge. The details supplied by Snorri of that battle, he remarks, "are confirmed by the *Chronicle,* at any rate insofar as the two accounts emphasize that Harold caught the Norsemen unawares whilst they were awaiting the hostages, whose surrender had been promised, and were expecting no further resistance in the north." Snorri's statement that the Norse lacked armor is another detail substantiated by the independent contemporary testimony of Marinius Scotus (Pertz, V, 559).

Carrying the argument even further against the rejection of Snorri's account of the battle, it may be observed that the similarities of his story to that of the Battle of Hastings may well be natural, for, as will be shown later, the English housecarls and the Norman knights fought in the same ways and with the same weapons. At Stamford Bridge, the English fought on horseback because the flat ground was ideal for such tactics. At Hastings, the housecarls dismounted to strengthen the fyrd on a position ideally suited to static defense. If Snorri falsified his story of Stamford Bridge, he disguised his deceit, where he might easily have faltered, by advancing the statement that the English were mounted at their first appearance.

The further charge that Snorri describes the Battle of Stamford Bridge in terms of thirteenth-century warfare is rejected by Richard Glover ("English Warfare in 1066," *English Historical Review,* January 1952), the first historian to emphasize the up-to-dateness of Anglo-Saxon methods of waging war. He points out that Snorri does not make the English horsemen charge with lances at rest, as thirteenth-century knights charged. His fidelity to truth is shown by the way he describes the battle according to accepted eleventh-century tactics, wherein the English horsemen were mounted javeliners who throw their lances, rather than true thirteenth-century cavalry. The tactics employed by the English at Stamford Bridge were similar to those used by the Normans at Hastings, as depicted in the Bayeux Tapestry. Snorri's accuracy in the military details of an earlier age is the best possible reason for accepting his story, claims Chambers. Snorri is therefore a dependable witness, both for the Battle of Stamford Bridge and for Anglo-Saxon methods of warfare.

Rounding off the argument, Warren Hollister (*Anglo-Saxon Military Institutions on the Eve of the Norman Conquest,* 1962), remarks that it would have been strange if the so-sophisticated system of English recruitment had provided such an ineffective military force as its detractors claim, and he believes that the eleventh-century Anglo-Saxon army must have included both a cavalry force and a large number of archers, as in fact Snorri states. The English, like the Normans, fought both on horseback and on foot. Our studies of the two great battles fought in England in the autumn of 1066 suggest that except against similarly equipped horsemen, the tactics of the mounted English housecarls and the Norman knights were singularly ineffective.

We left Hardrada and Tostig discussing whom the advancing army might be. They quickly recognized it as both hostile and commanded by King Harold though, for aught they knew, it could have been William and his Normans, flushed with a great victory over Harold.

Tostig recognized the danger at once. He suggested that the Norsemen retreat to their ships, "for there these horsemen will have no power over us." Hardrada rejected his counsel. Rather would he send swift messengers to Riccall, ordering the men there to come to his relief. Two youths, mounted on swift horses, galloped off.

The English army pours over the rise, deploying and moving rapidly down the slope toward the river. The Norsemen scattered on the York bank are driven back. Some reach safety across the bridge; others are caught with their backs to the river. Hardrada rejects, or does not consider, forming his line on the river bank, with sixty feet of water between him and his enemy. To fight across a river is not an accepted form of eleventh-century warfare. He uses the river only to delay the English advance, while he draws up his army three hundred yards in the rear, on the slope behind the town. He orders some Norsemen to hold the bridge.

The bridge which then existed lay probably about one hundred yards downstream from the present bridge which was built in 1727, when the old bridge, which may have been the original structure, became dangerous. The site was changed, probably to improve navigation by cutting a fresh channel, which eliminated the "shallows" by the old bridge. The position of the old bridge is confirmed both by the plan drawn by William Etty at the time of the change and by inherent probability. The river was fordable at the shallows, and there, in ancient times, were placed stepping-stones. Roads naturally converged at this point, and in Roman times a bridge was built. The building of the new bridge downstream required the road to be moved, as is suggested by the artificial nature of its present position entering the town's main street at right angles. Mr. F. W. Brooks (*The Battle of Stamford Bridge,* East Yorkshire Local History Society, 1963), who has made a detailed study of the ground, deduces another fact that supports this conclusion. The subsequent county boundary between the East and North Ridings of Yorkshire followed the old Roman road from York to Stamford Bridge, and it still meets the river at the weir, below the shallows. As there is no mention of the rectification of the boundary in 1727, it can be assumed that the Roman road always reached and crossed the river at this point. Colonel Burne (*More Battlefields of England,* 1952), on the other hand, prefers a site a little higher up the stream, which does not, as Mr. Brooks observes, affect the picture of the battle.

A valiant and nameless Norseman held up the English advance at the bridge for some time. This dramatic incident, which was unknown to Snorri, is related only by English chroniclers. Forty Englishmen fell beneath the Norse warrior's axe. Arrows were shot at him in vain, until at last an English soldier secured a boat, or a "salting tub," as another legend relates, and maneuvered his craft under the bridge, from where he was able to stab the heroic Norseman under his armor by thrusting his spear through the chinks between the bridge's timbers. This episode, records Mr. Brooks, lingered in local folk memory until recent times in the form of the "spear pies," made in the shape of a boat, which were eaten at a feast held on a date near the anniversary of the battle.

The delaying action at the bridge allowed Hardrada to draw up his warriors in a compact shield wall on the rising ground, which is known to this day as "Battle Flats," and where skeletons and weapons were unearthed in 1730.

The Norwegian King, states Snorri, bent the wings of his line back so that they met, forming a wide circle, equally thick all round, shield to shield, both in the front and rear ranks. The King and his retinue stood within the circle surrounded by a body of chosen men, grouped around the Land-Ravager. Earl Tostig, with his own retinue and a different banner, was at another place. "The army was arrayed in this way," says Snorri, "because the king knew that horsemen were accustomed to ride forward with great vigour but to turn back immediately," as soon as they had thrown their javelins, we may conclude. Hardrada ordered that his own and Tostig's attendants should ride to those parts of the circle where their presence was most required. "And our bowmen," he said, "shall be near to us; and they who stand in the first rank shall set the spear-shaft on the ground, and the spear-point against the horseman's breast, if he rides at them. And those who stand in the second rank shall set the spear-point against the horse's breast." Hardrada's battle order indicate that he prepared to meet horsemen who were likely to ride up, discharge their javelins and turn away. He provided also for the contingency that they might actually charge against the shield wall, seeking to break it by thrusting with their spears.

Hardrada rode round his army to see how every part of it was drawn up. His black horse stumbled under him, so that he fell off, not an unlikely accident to be suffered by a sailor on horseback, riding a strange horse, one of those seized by the Norsemen on their advance from Riccall. Hardrada, remounting in haste, shrugged off the ill omen with a Norse proverb, "A fall is lucky for a traveller." The accident was witnessed by King Harold, who was advancing with his "immense army, both of cavalry and infantry," according to Snorri. "Do you know the stout man who fell from his horse, with the blue kirtle and the beautiful helmet?" he asked a Norse prisoner. "That is the King himself," the man replied. "A great man, and of stately appearance is he, but I think his luck has left him," remarked Harold.

King Harold spurred his horse forward. Accompanied by twenty well-armed housecarls, he rode up to the Norse shield wall. "Is Earl Tostig in the army?" called one of the horsemen. The Earl acknowledged his presence. The horseman shouted again, "Thy brother, King Harold, sends thee salutation, with the message that you shall have the whole of Northumbria; and rather than you should not submit to him, he will give you the third part of his kingdom to rule over along with himself." To this improbable offer, Tostig is said to have replied: "This is something different from the enmity and scorn he offered last winter; and if this had been offered then it would have saved many a man's life who is now dead, and it would have been better for the Kingdom of England. But, if I accept this offer, what will he give King Harald Sigurdsson for his trouble?"

The horseman replied, "He will give him seven feet of English ground, or as much more as he may be taller than other men." "Then," said Tostig, "go now and tell King Harold to get ready for battle, for never shall the Norsemen say with truth that Earl Tostig left King Harald Sigurdsson to join his enemies, when he came to fight in England. We shall rather die together with honor, or gain England by a victory."

The horseman rode away. "Who was the man who spoke so well?" inquired Hardrada of Tostig. "That was King Harold," replied the Earl. "That was far too long concealed from me," said the King, and declared that had he known, Harold would not have been allowed to go away unharmed. "I would rather he should be my murderer than I his, if one of us is to die," exclaimed Tostig. Hardrada turned to his comrades with the remark that the King of the English was but a small man, but he stood well in his stirrups.

This famous dialogue may well be mythical, but on the other hand it may have some basis in fact.

The battle began. Snorri tells the story:

> The Englishmen made a hot assault upon the Northmen, who sustained it bravely. It was no easy matter for the English to ride against the Northmen on account of their spears; therefore they rode in a circle around them. And the fight at first was but loose and light, as long as the Northmen kept their order of battle; for although the English rode hard against the Northmen, they gave way again immediately, as they could do nothing against them. Now when the Northmen thought they perceived that the enemy were making but weak assaults, they set after them, and would drive them into flight; but when they had broken their shield-rampart the Englishmen rode up from all sides, and threw arrows and spears on them. Now when King Harald Sigurdsson saw this, he went into the fray where the greatest clash of weapons was; and there was a sharp conflict, in which many people fell on both sides. King Harald then was in a rage, and ran out in front of the array, and hewed down with both hands; so that neither helmet nor armour could withstand him, and all who were nearest gave way before him. It as then very near with the English that they had taken to flight. So says Arnor, the earls' skald:
>
> Where battle-storm was ringing,
> Where arrow-cloud was singing,

> Harald stood there,
> Of armour bare,
> His deadly sword still swinging.
> The foeman feel its bite;
> His Norsemen rush to fight,
> Danger to share
> With Harald there,
> Where steel on steel was ringing.

At this decisive moment, when the fate of the battle hangs by a thread, Hardrada is struck by an arrow in the windpipe. He falls to the ground mortally wounded, and all those who have charged with him are killed. Tostig takes the royal position by the Land-Ravager. Both armies reform their array, and there is a pause in the fighting:

> The army stands in hushed dismay
> Stilled is the clamour of the fray

sings the Norseman Thiodolf as the two armies rest to do honor, as it were, to the fall of one so mighty.

Before the battle recommences, Harold repeats his offer of peace to Tostig, promising quarter to the Norsemen who are still alive. They shout that they would rather fall, one across the other, than accept quarter from the English. Both armies utter their war cries, and the battle is rejoined. The renewed English assault culminates in the fall of Tostig, whose death at this stage may be assumed from the course of events.

At this moment, the Norse reinforcements, the contingent from Riccall commanded by Eystein Orre, march up, clad in full armor and suffering from exhaustion because of the haste they had made from the ships. They are scarcely fit to fight. They become furious, seized by berserker rage; they do not guard themselves with their shields while they stand upright. The conflict is so fierce that it is remembered in Norse legend as "Orre's storm." At last the Norsemen throw off their coats of ring mail. The English can then lay their blows on them. Many fall from weariness and die without wounds. Thus relates Snorri:

> . . . almost all the chief men fell amongst the Norway people. This happened towards evening, and then it went, as one might expect, that all had not the same fate, for many fled, and were lucky

> enough to escape in various ways; and darkness fell before the slaughter was altogether ended.

Snorri records the story of one such escape, an episode that, as has been remarked, shows the racial affinity between a Norseman and a man of northern England, who were able to understand each other's tongues:

> Styrkar, King Harald Sigurdsson's marshal, a gallant man, escaped upon a horse, on which he rode away in the evening. It was blowing a cold wind, and Styrkar had not much other clothing upon him but his shirt, and had a helmet on his head, and a drawn sword in his hand. As soon as his weariness was over, he began to feel cold. A waggoner met him in a lined skin-coat. Styrkar asks him, "Wilt thou sell thy coat, friend?"
>
> "Not to thee," says the peasant, "thou art a Northman; that I can hear by thy tongue."
>
> Styrkar replies, "If I were a Northman, what wouldst thou do?"
>
> "I would kill thee," replied the peasant, "but, as ill luck would have it, I have no weapon just now by me that would do it."
>
> Then Styrkar says, "As you can't kill me, friend, I shall try if I can't kill you." And with that he swung his sword, and struck him on the neck, so that his head came off. He then took the skin-coat, sprang on his horse, and rode down to the strand.

Other Norsemen may have regained the fleet at Riccall or found refuge among their kindred in the northern counties. The nameless Irish king died in the battle, and Godred of Iceland survived. He fled to the Isle of Man, of which he became the conqueror, waging a successful war against Dublin and Leinster. The body of Tostig, disfigured by the wounds dealt by an Englishman's two-edged axe, his head cloven to the chin, was identified by a distinctive mark and carried to York, where it was interred. The easily recognized body of the giant Hardrada was found, surrounded by the corpses of the men he had slain with his two-handed axe, and a year later it was transported to Norway, where it was buried in a church he had built at Nidaros.

The measure of the English victory is shown by King Harold's treatment of Hardrada's son Olaf, who, with the two earls of Orkney, had remained with the fleet. Harold could afford to be generous. He had no more to fear from the Norsemen. He allowed Olaf to sail to Norway with sufficient ships to carry the survivors of the battle. The ships numbered only 24 out of the three hundred that had brought the hosts of the North. Olaf and his chiefs came to York, where they gave hostages and swore oaths that they would forever keep peace and friendship with England. This informal international treaty is honored to this day. In Hardrada's longship was found his great ingot of gold, a king's ransom in treasure. It remained in Harold's possession for less than three weeks.

Harold had won a great victory. His impetuous dash to the North had paid off. He had met in battle and defeated one of the two invaders who threatened his kingdom. He had annihilated the Norsemen's army and had captured their fleet. The English losses must have been severe. Harold's "immense army" had dwindled considerably. As urgent as it was that he should return to the South, such a march was clearly impossible for several days, and some time was occupied by the negotiations with Olaf and the resettlement of the North under the two earls, Edwin and Morcar, who, if they fought at Stamford Bridge, survived the day. Nor could Harold abstain from the customary celebration of the victory. He was seated at the banquet in York, possibly on 1 October, when a thegn from Sussex, travel-stained and weary, burst in upon him with the news that William of Normandy had landed at Pevensey on the morning of 28 September.

Nine

The Sea

Shortly after the westerly gale had carried the Norman fleet to St. Valéry at the mouth of the Somme estuary, an anti-cyclone moving in from the Atlantic pulled the wind round to the north, but it still blew hard. It may have been accompanied by heavy, squally rain. Modern meteorologists might have predicted that these adverse winds were likely to persist until pressure rose generally or the anti-cyclone moved farther eastwards. If William consulted the local fishermen, they might have told him from their experience that a strong wind from the north at that time of the year would probably blow for some time, and they may have warned that the season of equinoctial gales was due. Their advice could not have been cheering. William was champing to be off. His spies informed him that Harold had abandoned his watch, disbanded his militia and sent his fleet to London. The coast was clear. It was the golden moment to invade England, before Harold could reprovision and remobilize the fyrd and the fleet. In the next few weeks the Normans could land unopposed. William hoped to bring Harold to quick battle, but he did not want to fight on the beaches, for at that moment his invasion would be most vulnerable.

William had chosen Pevensey for his landing place. The little Sussex port offered certain advantages over the alternative sites, Chichester Harbour and Southampton Water, eighty and one hundred miles to the west respectively. Pevensey was then a tiny islet, a narrow peninsula jutting into a vast lagoon of marsh and stream, which extended from the Downs on the west to Hastings on the east. Hastings was a considerable port, connected to London by a road intersected seven miles from the coast, at a place named Hoar Apple Tree, by an east-west highway. The capture of Hastings was an essential prelude to the campaign. William planned to land some miles from the town; he needed time and space in which to disembark his army and to build up a striking force. Pevensey, remote and girt by deep, watery channels and clusters of low islands, provided a solution to William's particular problem, how to get his horses ashore. The indented coastline was protected from westerly gales by the massive rampart of Beachy Head, and there were docks both at "Pevensae," as the Bayeux Tapestry spells the name, and North-Eye, which had been built by the Romans to ship iron ore from Andredsweald, the great forest that stretched between the South and North Downs. The Romans built a fort at Pevensey, which they called Andredcaster, and they made it one of the strong points of the south "Saxon shore." In 491, after the Roman withdrawal, it had been besieged and taken by the Saxon chieftains Aella and Asa, who, the *Saxon Chronicle* records, "slew all that dwelt therein, so that not one Briton was left alive."

Pevensey lay only sixty miles across the sea from St. Valéry, but as long as the wind blew from the north, it was as remote as the North Pole. William chafed at the delay. The barons, he saw, were becoming weary of waiting. The Duke noted dangerous signs of dissatisfaction and disruption. He could not keep his volunteer and mercenary army forever. His eyes sought the weathercock on the tower of the Minster. Day after day it pointed to the north. For fifteen days the sky continued cloudy, the weather cold and rainy. By 20 September, possibly, William may have learned of Hardrada's landing and of Harold's impulsive dash to the north. The news stretched his patience to the utmost. Whatever was the strength of the Norse invasion, it provided a heaven-sent diversion, for, the moment the Normans could transport themselves across the Channel, Harold would be committed to a war on two fronts.

William prayed for good weather, imploring God that the wind might be favorable. Kneeling in fervent supplication in the church, he had an inspiration. His eyes lighted upon the shrine of St. Valéry the Confessor, the beloved of God. He persuaded the monks to bring out the shrine containing the wonder-working body of the saint, their patron. Led by the abbot himself, they carried it in solemn procession and set it on a carpet on the plain outside the church. There it was exposed to the view of the whole army. The bringing out of the body of the saint made a deep impression. "And all," states Wace, "came praying the Holy relics that they might be allowed to pass over the sea." The barons, he says, offered so much money that the relics were buried beneath it. The prayers and costly gifts were soon rewarded. "And from that day forth they had good weather and a fair wind," records Wace. The longed-for south wind began to blow early on the morning of Wednesday, 27 September. "All raised their hands and voices in thanks to Heaven," says William of Poitiers. There was a tumult of joy. The days of weary waiting were over; England and her spoils lay ahead. The dread of the unknown, the perils of the sea, the fear of Harold's soldiers, all were dissipated in the delirium of excitement, of glorious anticipation. Dark doubts were dispelled by renewed belief in the rightness of the cause upon which the army was about to cross the sea. William did not know whom he would have to fight for the throne of England, Harold and his Saxons or Hardrada and his Norsemen, who, still unknown to him, had met at Stamford Bridge two days before. He gave orders for immediate embarkation.

The soldiers rushed to the shore, all determined to be first on board, each man eager to outstrip the others, one calling for his knight, another for his companion, all forgetful alike of followers and friends, so anxious were they to reach the ships, so fearful were they of being left behind. So excited were the soldiers that many forgot to bring the stores and provisions they had so carefully collected. The Tapestry shows that others marched to the ships carrying on their shoulders spears and swords, helmets and hauberks, the heavy coats of mail slung on poles, each requiring two men to carry. Many men shouldered skins and casks of wine; a few yoked themselves to wagons loaded with casks and spears arranged in racks. The sailors dragged the ships to the sea, using pulleys fastened to posts fixed in the water, set up masts and unfurled sails. The harbor resounded with the music of pipes, zitterns, drums and cymbals. The strident voices of trumpets, calling the men to England, resounded from the low heights surrounding the estuary. From their camps on the hills came the knights riding their warhorses.

Two problems yet await our discussion; the number of Normans and their allies who crossed the Channel and how William carried his horses over the sea.

The strength of the armies with which William invaded England and against which Harold fought, is variously stated by contemporary chroniclers. The English writers minimize, not unnaturally, and the Normans proudly inflate the size of Harold's army, exaggerating their own numbers. William of Poitiers says that the Normans numbered sixty thousand men. The term *sexcenti,* which he uses, was then a common phrase for a generally large number. We find William, after the Conquest, creating sixty thousand knight's fees and meeting sixty thousand vassals at Salisbury. Other Norman writers say that their army numbered one hundred thousand men. These figures are wild exaggerations. The written authorities are not reliable guides. It is possible, however, to deduce the relative strengths from other sources of information, from the number of Norman ships and the length of the battle ridge at Hastings.

Benoît de St. More says that the Norman fleet numbered three thousand vessels. Wace relates that he was told by his father, who lived at the time, that there were seven hundred less four ships and many smaller craft. Ordericus Vitalis records that 782 ships were promised by the great barons and the bishops, a number that, if the quotas were not fully filled, approximates Wace's 696. The majority of these vessels were specially built to transport the invasion army, and there is no reason to think that these ships were constructed to any particular specifications, although they were all of the same type, open-decked longships, on the pattern of the Norse ship.

But which type of Norse ship? The Vikings built both warships and cargo boats, which were called "knorrs" (*The Ship,* Bjorn Landstrom, 1961). Unlike the warship, no example of the trader has survived, unless the Oseberg ship, found in 1903, was of that type. It had no deck other than floor boards, which were raised into shallow platforms at prow and stern, and it had less "rake" than the Gokstadt ship. Mr. F. W. Brooks (*The English Naval Forces 1199–1272,* 1932) identifies the ships depicted in the Tapestry as "esneccas," developed from the Norse warship, the "snekkjur," and he describes them as medium-sized longships. The largest vessel depicted in the Tapestry has thirteen shields slung over the bulwark. If there were that number of cross benches, seating four armed men each, its capacity was fifty-two men. Many of the ships may have been smaller, and there were also horses to carry.

The Tapestry shows that the horse transports varied in size. One ship carries nine horses and eight men, another four horses and five men. In the list of ships donated, one, given by Bishop Remigius, provided accommodation for twenty knights, another, furnished by the Abbot of St. Ouen, for five knights only. In other cases the ratio varied from three and one-half to one and one-half per ship. Three knights and their horses, with their esquires, seems to have been a common number. Thus, if the "infantry" transports carried an average of twenty-five men each and the "horse" transports eight men and horses, and if we suppose that there were 296 ships carrying men-at-arms and bowmen and four hundred transporting horses and their riders, we arrive at the figure of 7,300 infantry and 3,200 mounted men, about 10,500 men in all. As some were sailors and camp followers, it is reasonable to conclude that the effective strength of William's army was about 7,500 men. To ship 10,000 men and 3,000 horses across the Channel in 1066 was a considerable achievement, and that figure was not bettered in the next three hundred years by either Edward III in 1346 or Henry V in 1415–1417. In 1254, a ship capable of transporting thirty men is spoken of in Eccleston's *Antiquities* as of extraordinary magnitude. In 1346 the expedition to Calais comprised 783 ships, which could carry twenty men each. By 1360 the largest ship carried only forty-four men.

This figure of 7,500 effective Norman soldiers is singularly confirmed by the estimate of the number of men engaged on both sides at the Battle of Hastings, where Harold positioned his army on the ridge. General J. F. C. Fuller (*Decisive Battles of the Western World,* Vol. I, 1954) calculates that, "if Harold drew up his army in a phalanx of ten ranks deep to allow two feet frontage for each man in the first rank—the shield wall—and three feet frontage for those in the nine rear ranks, then on a 600-yard front his total strength would be 6,300 men, and if in twelve ranks, 7,500." All commentators agree that the English army was equal to, or slightly greater in numbers than, its Norman opponent, of whom about 3,000 were horsemen.

How did William load, transport across the Channel and unload that number of horses? He embarked his army first at the mouth of the River Dive and then in the estuary of the Somme. Both rivers were tidal, their banks steep and precipitous.

William undoubtedly discussed the problem of horse transport with the contingent of knights who came from Sicily. Whether or not they advised that he copy the Byzantine method of constructing ships, the sides of which let down to enable armed horsemen to ride ashore, the Bayeux Tapestry makes it certain that the Normans did not adopt that method in 1066. If they built such special ships, it is inconceivable that the designer of the Tapestry would have failed to remark their ingenuity by depicting the horsemen riding ashore ready for battle.

There seem to be only three other methods by which the Normans could have embarked their horses in open ships. In the opinion of a friend of the author, who is both a yachtsman and a horseman, as well as a keen student of military history, the Normans beached their ships at low tide, led their horses aboard and awaited the rising tide to refloat them. This theory is open to the fatal objection that it left to hazard the most vital part of the operation, disembarkation, possibly on a hostile shore. The Normans planned too carefully to take such a risk. It is possible that the Normans used slings to embark horses. If they employed that ingenious method, it is strange that the Tapestry fails to record it.

Though the Italian authorities give no hint of its nature, they indicate that the Normans of Sicily had found a method of transporting horses, one that they employed frequently and successfully. Plate 46 of the Tapestry, which illustrates the disembarkation of horses at Pevensey, provides a clue to how this may have been done. Two horses, led by one man, are shown jumping into shallow water from the beached ship. The hindleg of one is still over the gunwale, its hoof resting apparently on an unseen foredeck. This picture suggests that the Normans built within each ship a platform or deck and a gangway, up and down which the horses were led, to and from the depth of five feet below the gunwale.

According to this theory, they dug a number of ramps in the banks of the two rivers where they loaded horses. These ramps were cut downward and sideways, parallel to the bank, and they were levelled off at intervals, to provide flat loading points, corresponding to the positions of the ships at different tide levels. Forty such ramps may have been made, each designed for loading ten ships in rotation. When the order to embark was given, each horse was led by its rider or its esquire down the ramp until its hooves were level with the gunwale.

The horse was then led across the gunwale onto the platform and down the slatted gangway toward the bow, where it was secured by hurdles. More horses were brought aboard until the ship was loaded, then it was moved into the channel and moored, making way for another transport. The Norman horses were trained for war, and were accustomed to their riders and their esquires. Some, no doubt, were nervous and difficult to handle. Others were docile and easy. The operation would have been difficult when the sea was rough, simple when it was calm. Eight horses could have been loaded into a ship in one hour. If each ramp served ten ships, three thousand horses could have been embarked within ten hours.

On 27 September the wind changed to the south in time for the Normans to embark their army by evening and to sail that night. Common sense suggests that they sailed with the tide, which that night was high in the estuary of the Somme at about 10:30 P.M. (G.M.T.), according to calculations made by the Hydrographic Department of the British Admiralty, which computed the tidal patterns for September 1066 for me in 1964. Thus, if the wind changed early in the day, as both probability and the sources suggest, the Normans had at least ten hours in which to load their horse transports.

William was busy all day, supervising the embarkation and attending to those little details that would ensure success, vehemently urging on the laggards, cautioning the overeager. He was about to set out on a hazardous enterprise, of which no man could forecast the outcome. "He put his fortunes to extreme hazard," remarks Professor Douglas (*William the Conqueror,* 1964). Having seen that all was in order, he went to the Minster to pray. There he was accosted by a priest, an amateur soothsayer, who assured him that his voyage would be prosperous and that he would win England without a blow. Harold would bow to him and become his liege man. The priest went aboard his transport, and William embarked on his own ship *Mora,* the gift of his duchess, at the prow of which stood the figure of a child cast in brass, bearing an arrow with a bent bow. A herald rode along the shore calling out the Duke's last commands. The ships were to keep together, each was to bear a light and follow the huge lantern slung at the mast of the *Mora.*

Fearing that if the fleet reached the opposite shore before daylight, the army might have to disembark in confusion, the Duke ordered that the ships were to tarry awhile at the dead hour of the night and await signals from his ship.

The trumpets sounded, and the fleet headed out to sea, led by the *Mora,* the face of the brazen child turned toward England. "And thither he looked," says Wace, "as though he was about to shoot, so that whichever way the ship went, he seemed to shoot onwards." It was very dark. The heavens were clouded and the moon hidden, the sea flecked by a thousand dancing lights. It was the greatest armada of conquest to cross the English Channel until the operation staged 878 years later by the Americans and the British.

The ships halted and rested in the early hours of the morning. Shortly before daylight, the trumpet called from the *Mora,* and the fleet sailed again, following the blazing beacon at her mast. The lightly laden flagship soon outstripped the others. When dawn broke, the Duke's ship was alone. At William's bidding, a sailor climbed the mast to see if the other vessels were in sight. He could see nothing but sea and sky, he cried. William called a halt. To assuage the apprehension of his companions, he commanded a large repast to be served. A bumper of spiced wine was broached. The Duke dined in good spirits, according to the chroniclers of the voyage, as if he were in a room of his own house. He bade his men be of good heart, assuring them that their comrades would soon overtake them. God, in whose cause they were setting out, would watch over the safety of all the host. And so it came about. The sailor, ordered aloft again, reported four ships in sight. Then he called that he saw what looked like a forest upon the waves, a multitude of masts clustered together. William's heart was lifted up in thankfulness. The south wind still blew. The fleet was well across the Channel. With the coming of full daylight, the lantern on the *Mora* was extinguished, and the fleet coming over the horizon followed her checkered sails. Only two ships were in any peril during the voyage, perhaps because they were overloaded, says Wace. About 7 A.M. the low outline of the Sussex coast loomed ahead.

The Norman chroniclers state that William landed at Pevensey about 9 A.M. on St. Michael's Eve, 28 September. The fleet was not allowed to scatter, and all the ships steered for the same point, casting anchor as

The battlefield of Hastings, specially photographed to the author's specifications, by Meridian Air Maps Ltd., of Lancing, Sussex, taken at about the time of year the battle took place. The English were drawn up on the ridge, now occupied by the Abbey buildings, their right flank resting on the ravine of the stream, clearly visible; their left flank at the triangle of buildings to the right of the church. The Normans deployed down the slopes of Telham Hill (right of picture) and across the present east-west road (Battle to Bexhill). They advanced up the slopes now obscured by trees, in the center of which still stands the "hillock," just north of the pond.

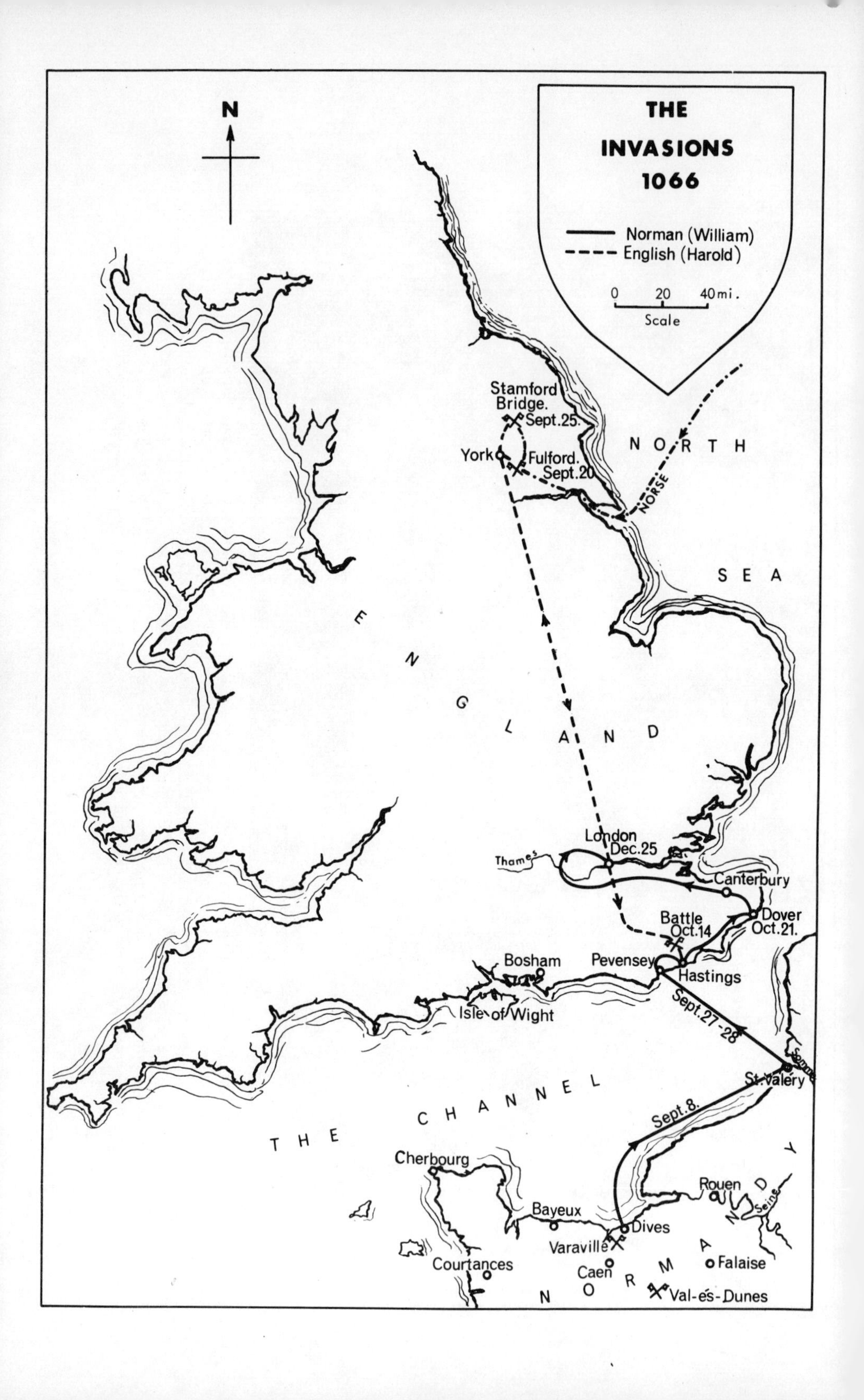

N
THE INVASIONS 1066
Norman (William)
English (Harold)
0 20 40mi.
Scale
Stamford Bridge.
Sept.25.
York
Fulford.
Sept.20
NORTH
NORSE
SEA
E N G L A N D
London
Dec.25
Thames
Canterbury
Dover
Oct.21.
Battle
Oct.14
Pevensey
Hastings
Bosham
Isle of Wight
Sept.27-28
Somme
St.Valery
THE CHANNEL
Sept.8.
Cherbourg
Rouen
Seine
Bayeux
Dives
Varaville
Courtances
Caen
Falaise
Val-es-Dunes
N O R M A N D Y

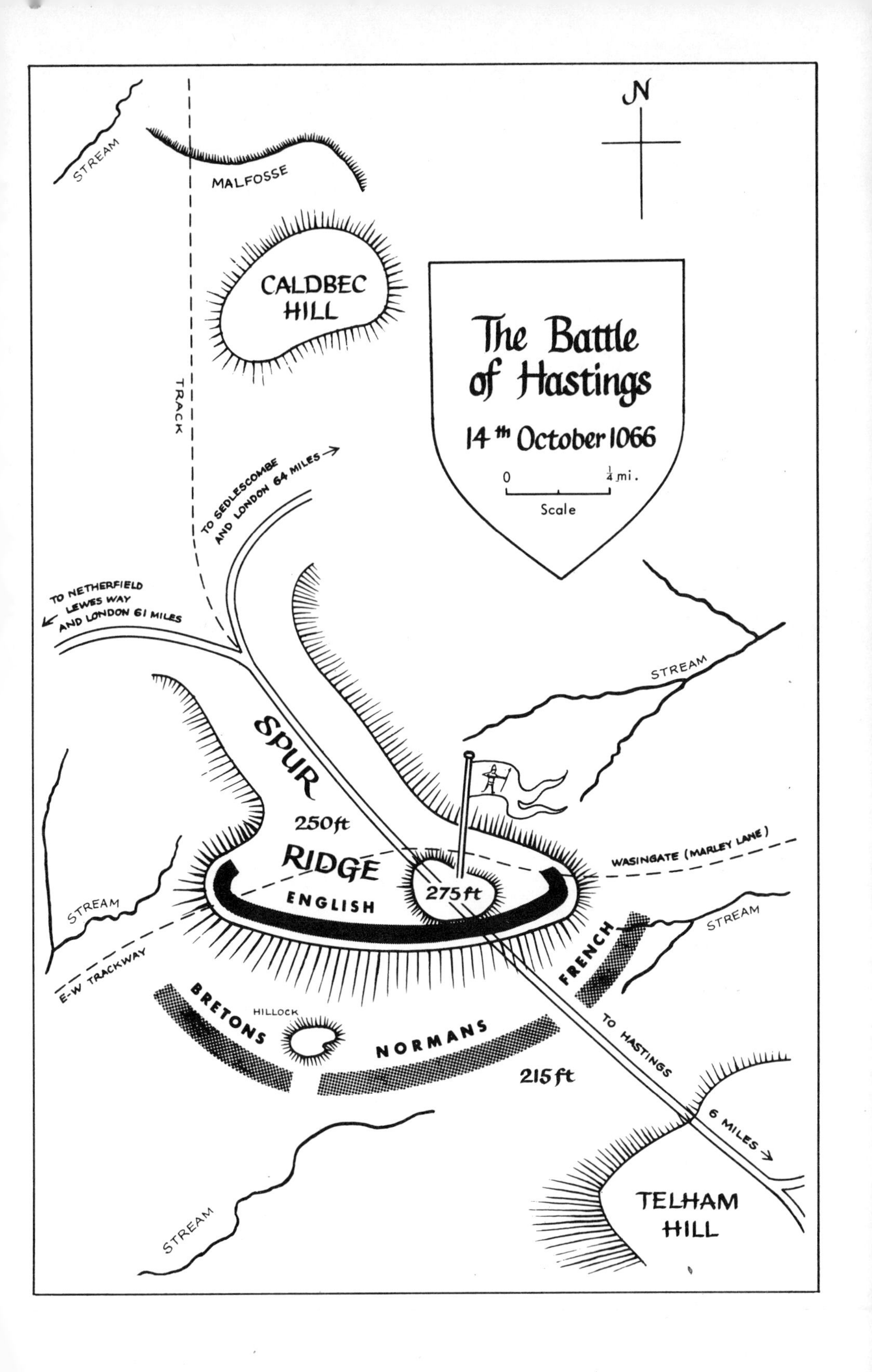

The Battle of Hastings
14th October 1066
0
1/4 mi.
Scale
N
STREAM
MALFOSSE
CALDBEC HILL
TRACK
TO SEDLESCOMBE AND LONDON 64 MILES
TO NETHERFIELD LEWES WAY AND LONDON 61 MILES
STREAM
SPUR
250ft
RIDGE
ENGLISH
275ft
WASINGATE (MARLEY LANE)
STREAM
STREAM
FRENCH
E-W TRACKWAY
BRETONS
HILLOCK
NORMANS
215ft
TO HASTINGS
6 MILES
TELHAM HILL
STREAM

The English drawn up on the ridge, the Normans and their allies deploying for the first assault, the French on the right, the Normans in the center, the Bretons on the left.

The first assault, the Bretons reaching the English line first.

The Normans feign flight, drawing the English militia after them, who are cut down by the liers in wait.

About 4 P.M., the Normans, despairing of victory, order the archers to fire high, while the knights charge in under their arrows.

The final assault on the ridge.

near together as might be in or about the haven of Pevensey. A wave of fighting men, preceded by archers with their bows bent ready for action, their quivers full of arrows at their sides, "all shaven and shorn, all clad in short garments, ready to attack, to shoot, to wheel, to skirmish," waded ashore, led by the Duke himself. As William descended from the *Mora,* his foot slipped, and he fell with both hands to the ground. A low cry of fear arose from the army at this ill omen. William passed off the accident with ready wit. "By the Splendor of God," he cried, "I have taken possession of my kingdom; the earth of England is in my hands." The soldiers fanned out over the marshes, scouring the shore. A few peasants were seen fleeing in the distance, quitting their homes and driving off their cattle. Some of the fugitives took refuge in a cemetery. Domesday records that 25 of the 52 burgesses of the town were put to the sword. William ordered the trumpets to sound; no answering call came. No army stood ready to oppose the Normans. The soldiers occupied Pevensey, and William ordered the knights to disembark. The esquires led the horses up the gangways and onto the raised platforms; the horses jumped into the shallow water and were led ashore. Sergeants and esquires carried the saddles and armor. The knights donned their hauberks, laced their helmets, hung their shields at their necks, girt their swords and mounted their horses, forming in full battle array. The high "spring" tide, which was full by 11:15 A.M. and which carried the ships high up the shore, made it possible for the operation to be accomplished quickly and efficiently. When the soldiers and knights had disembarked, the sailors dragged the ships onto dry land, furled the sails and unshipped the masts.

After the landing had been made, carpenters and engineers came from the ships, carrying materials shaped and framed beforehand, cut and ready for quick assembly, for the construction of a defensive work placed within the shell of the old Roman fort overlooking the harbor, the crumbling walls of which stand to this day. The soldiers lit fires and cooked their meat. The Duke, his barons and their knights had plenty to eat, for they had brought ample provisions. "All ate and drank enough, and were right glad they were ashore," remarks Wace.

After he had refreshed himself, the Duke inquired about the soothsayer who had predicted a good passage. The priest had suffered a misadventure and had been drowned in one of the lost ships, a sailor told him. "No great deal could he have known," observed William, and he remarked: "A poor diviner must he be about me, who could predict nought about himself. If the things to come were known to him, he might well have foreseen his own death. Foolish is he who trusts in a diviner," William warned his companions, "who takes heed for others but forgets himself; who knows the end of other men's work and cannot discern the term of his own life."

Wace's reference to two ships lost during the crossing raises the question of what happened to them. Although they may have sunk from being overloaded or capsized at the landing, it is possible that they were swept down the coast, reaching Romney, where their crews were killed. It is difficult otherwise to account for an incident recorded by William of Poitiers, who states that after his victory at Hastings, William took vengeance on the citizens of Romney "for the slaughter of his men," although it is also possible that the men slain may have been a foraging party sent out from Hastings.

The Norman landing was observed by a Saxon thegn, who was alarmed by the cries and lamentations of the peasants who saw the fleet arrive. He knew that it was the Normans who came and that their object was to conquer England. He posted himself behind a hill (which suggests that he was some miles from Pevensey) so that they should not see him and watched the arrival of the great fleet. He saw the archers come forth from the ships and the knights follow. He saw the carpenters with their axes and the host of people and troops. He saw the men throw the materials for the fort out of the ships. He saw them build up and enclose the fort and dig the fosse around it. He saw them land the shields and armor. And as he beheld all this, his spirit was troubled; he girt on his sword and took his lance, and he set out to find King Harold to tell him the news. He rested late and rose early, riding by night and by day, seeking the King.

The Normans remained only one day at Pevensey, according to the chroniclers. Leaving a garrison to guard the fleet, they marched to Hastings. This was easier said than done, for Pevensey lay in a vast lagoon of marsh and water, and the only access to the port is believed to have been from the west, by a causeway from Polegate and Hailsham. If this is true, William could have marched his army to Hastings, which lay to the east, only by a circuitous route, via Hurstmonceux and Ninfield, a journey that would have taken several days. The late Rector of Ninfield, the Rev. E. H. Rudkin ("Where Did William Land?" *Sussex County Magazine,* Vol. II, 1928) envisages another causeway, running northeastward from Pevensey, via Watling, to Ninfield. He records also the local tradition that the Normans, or some of them, landed to the east of Pevensey at Bulver Haven, near modern Bexhill, and elsewhere among the many little havens within the marshes. The inaccessibility of Pevensey, otherwise so suitable for the Norman invasion, carried its disadvantages, and it may well be that having seized Hastings with his advance guard, William shipped his army to that port from Pevensey.

The citizens of Hastings surrendered without striking a blow. William established his headquarters on a hill that stood between two valleys leading northward, and there he built a wooden castle surrounded by a ditch and a palisade, conscripting local labor for this urgent task, which the Tapestry shows being accomplished. The fleet was brought into the harbor at Hastings, and William reviewed his army. He settled down to await the coming of Harold.

Within a few days, by early October, William must have heard rumors of the Battle of Stamford Bridge and its result. Harold, he believed, was at York, 250 miles away, his army considerably reduced in strength by the great victory he had won. Whatever were Harold's losses, he could raise another army, greater in number than the Norman host. But that would take time. William's counsellors may have urged a quick dash to London before Harold could return from the North. The Normans would have to march only 70 miles, and 190 miles lay between York and London. William refused to change his plan to bring Harold to battle near the coast. He set out to provoke Harold to rashness, to tempt him south; the Normans ravaged the countryside around Hastings, pillaging, killing and burning. Sussex was part of Harold's Earldom of Wessex, the victims his own people. Refugees fled northward to inform their lord of the havoc and destruction. The ravaging of southeastern Sussex was done with completeness and singleness of purpose. The Bayeux Tapestry shows parties of Normans scouring the countryside, rounding up cattle and setting fire to a house, from which a woman and a child are being driven. When the Domesday Survey was made twenty years later, the devastation was still evident. Fourteen villages around Hastings were described as *vastatumfuit.* During the two weeks of Norman occupation, the value of the manors of Catsfield and Hooe fell from £4 to £1 and from £25 to £6, respectively. A whole village declined in value from one hundred to twenty shillings, and another was rendered completely valueless.

William himself, accompanied by twenty-five knights, rode out to gain information about the neighborhood and its inhabitants. William of Poitiers reports: "Because of the roughness of the ground he had to return on foot, a matter doubtless for laughter, but if the episode is not devoid of humour, it nonetheless deserved serious praise, for the duke came carrying on his shoulder, besides his own hauberk, that of William Fitz-Osbern, one of his companions. This man was famed for his bodily strength and courage, but it was the duke who relieved him in his necessity of the weight of his armour."

The outcome of the Battle of Stamford Bridge was confirmed to William in a message sent by the late King's staller, Robert Fitz-Wymarc, who added a warning. "King Harold," he said, "has just given battle to his brother and to the king of Norway, who is reputed to be the greatest warrior under Heaven, and he has killed both of them in one fight, and has destroyed their mighty armies. Heartened by this success, he now hastens toward you at the head of innumerable troops, all well-equipped for war, and against them your own warriors will prove of no more account than a pack of curs. You are accounted a wise man, and at home you have hitherto acted prudently both in peace and war. Now therefore take care for your own safety lest your boldness lead you into a peril from which you will not escape. My advice to you is to remain within your entrenchments and not at present to offer battle."

The opinion of a Norman, long resident in England, that the Normans were no match for the English is striking proof that the Anglo-Saxon army was not the fossilized, antiquated force its detractors maintain. The caution with which William hugged the coast for two weeks after his landing, building fortresses to cover his forced re-embarkation should the need arise, indicates the marked respect that the Norman Duke accorded his formidable opponent. Nonetheless, William made an audacious reply to the gloomy Norman. He told the messenger: "Although it would have been better for your master not to have mingled insults with his message, nevertheless I thank him for his advice. But say this also to him; I have no desire to protect myself behind any ramparts, but I intend to give battle to Harold as soon as possible. With the aid of God I would not hesitate to oppose him with my own brave men, if I had only ten thousand of these, instead of the sixty thousand I now command."

William knew that Harold was on his way south. His reference to his "sixty thousand" men may have been bombast. It could have been shrewd, for the tale might be carried to Harold when he reached London.

The thegn from Sussex found Harold at York. He told him what he had seen, a great fleet, a countless host, horsemen, archers and men-at-arms. The Normans had built a fort and fenced it with a palisade. Harold cursed his ill luck. At the moment of triumph over Hardrada, the news of William's landing was a shattering blow. While he rejoiced in a victory over one enemy, the other had stolen upon him unawares. It would have been better, Harold exclaimed, to have given Tostig all he asked, so that he himself could have remained in the South. If he had been stationed on the Sussex coast, the Normans would never have made their landing. They would have been driven back into the sea, or they would have perished on English ground. "But the mischance was the will of the King of Heaven," lamented Harold. He could not be everywhere at the same time. It was not too late. He could still defeat William.

Harold called a council of war. He told his men of William's landing. He warned them of the horrors that would follow if the Norman invasion succeeded. He announced his determination to march south at once. A loud shout of unanimous consent rose from the assembly. Every man pledged his faith to acknowledge no other king but Harold. Before he left York, Harold committed the command of northern England to Sheriff Merlswegen. Neither Edwin nor Morcar accompanied the army south. Their troops had been severely defeated at Fulford, and they were probably in no condition to fight again for some months. The march to the south was speeded by further news, borne by a churl from Hastings; the army of Normans, Frenchmen and Bretons, whom no man could number, was ravaging far and wide. Harold's liege men were being slain; their widows, their sons, their daughters and their flocks and herds were the prey of strangers.

Harold left York about 2 October. He rode at the head of his housecarls, their numbers thinned by their great victory over the Norsemen. Behind straggled the remnant of the fyrd of the southern counties, some on horseback, many on foot. As the march proceeded, they lagged farther and farther behind. The army, it has been suggested, was disgruntled because Harold had not shared the spoil from the Norse fleet. Ignoring established custom, he had given it intact into the care of Archbishop Eldred. He did so, probably, for good reason; at the moment of crisis he needed all the wealth he could amass, and he may have wished to prevent his men from marching from one battlefield to another laden with plunder.

The King sent messengers galloping ahead, summoning his array, the fyrd of the Midlands and the western counties and the men of the South whom he had not called to the North, naming London as the trysting place. The men of England, says Wace, flocked to Harold's standard. He lists the army as assembling from such places as London, Kent, Hertford, Essex, Surrey, Sussex, Saint Edmund's and Suffolk, Norwich and Norfolk, Canterbury and Stamford, Bedford, Huntingdon, Northampton, York, Buckingham, Nottingham, Lindsey and Lincoln, Salisbury, Dorset, Bath and Somerset, Worcester, Winchester and Hampshire and Berkshire.

Who these men were, and their quality, are less certain. Some may have been the remnants of the select fyrd that had marched north in September; others were gallant volunteers who answered the King's call at the moment of need. Many were recruited en route. The majority were probably members of the greater fyrd, local levies, courageous men but ill trained and ill equipped. The men of London were led by Esegar, Sheriff of the Middle Saxons, and by ancient right they guarded the King and his standard.

Harold reached London on the night of 5 October or early next day, ten days after the Battle of Stamford Bridge and a week after the Norman landing. Impatient to bring William to battle, Harold was forced to wait while the army mustered. He remobilized the fleet and sent it to patrol the Channel. He made a pilgrimage to Waltham, where, kneeling in prayer before the altar, he vowed that if God gave him victory, he would further endow the abbey with gifts and lands and would look upon himself as God's ransomed servant, devoting himself to His special service forever. As he turned to depart, the canons and monks led him along the stately nave, flanked by a double row of massive columns, to the wonder-working relic, the Holy Rood of Waltham, before which he prostrated himself. Then, it was testified by the Sacrist Thurkill, the holy image bowed to the King, as if to say that his career was finished. In after days, many others who were present claimed to have witnessed the divine wonder.

Harold returned to London. He and William exchanged challenges. The authenticity of the surviving texts may be doubtful, but the general import is clear. Both Harold and William were making propaganda, the prelude to battle. William assumed the character of the legitimate claimant to the throne, the armed missionary of God, come to punish the perjurer. Harold claimed to be the national king, the people's choice. There are several versions of these interchanges of messages and of the order in which they were sent and received.

William accused Harold of forgetting his oath. King Edward had given him the kingdom. "Restore the kingdom you have seized," cried William. In his reply, Harold did not deny his oath. He had sworn it to obtain his freedom, he insisted. He had not done it of his free will. The strength had been on the Duke's side, and Harold had feared that, unless he did his pleasure, he would not return but would remain in Normandy forever. Nor did Harold deny King Edward's early promise to William; it had been cancelled by his later bequest. Ever since the days of the blessed Augustine, who first preached the Gospel to Englishmen, it had always been the law of England that a testament had no strength while the testator lived, for, up to the moment of his death, a man could revoke any disposition of his goods, which could not take effect until the breath was out of his body. Edward's promise made in 1051 had been rendered null and void by his dying nomination of Harold. Harold offered to recompense William for his trouble and give him safe conduct to return home. If he refused, Harold would meet him Saturday week and do battle with him.

Harold prepared to fulfill his offer of speedy battle. His brother Gyrth tried to turn him from his purpose. The advice was good; Harold was weary from his labors in the North; his army was not strong enough to justify undertaking a decisive battle. Then there was the matter of the oath Harold had sworn to William; it was not good that a man should fight the lord to whom he had done homage. He,

Gyrth, had no such scruple. He could go to battle with a clear conscience. Let the King not risk himself and jeopardize his kingdom on the chances of a single battle. Let Gyrth fight William. If he defeated the invader, the gain to England would be as great as if Harold overcame him. But if William overcame Gyrth, the loss to England would be far less. If Gyrth were defeated, Harold could still gather another army. Gyrth urged Harold to allow him to go forth with the troops already assembled, while the King waited until an even greater force had answered his summons. Gyrth reasoned wisely. In the words of Wace, he counselled his brother: "Whilst I go and fight the Normans, do you scour the country, burn the houses, destroy the villages, and carry off all stores and provisions, swine and goats and cattle; that they may find no food or anything whatever to subsist upon. Thus you may alarm and drive them back, for the duke must return to his own country if provisions for his army shall fail him." Harold refused to listen to his brother's advice, telling him: "Never will I harm an English village or an English home, nor will I harm the lands or goods of any Englishman. How can I do hurt to the folk who are put under me to govern? How can I plunder and harass those I would fain see thrive under my rule?"

What Harold should have done has been argued for centuries. Brave and courageous as he undoubtedly was, Harold was too impetuous to be a great military commander. Two weeks before, in September, he had fought a pitched battle, in which his army must have suffered severely. He had won it by an impulsive dash to the North, by a march that had taken the enemy by surprise. In October, he planned to repeat the tactic of impetuous assault, but the vital element of complete surprise was lacking. Harold played into William's hands; he hurried to Sussex, ill prepared and with only half his army, to fight a decisive battle when and where William desired. William had hoped he would, had expected he would. He banked on Harold's impetuosity. He knew him; he knew he was prone to rashness, too daring and overconfident. Those weaknesses outweighed, in William's estimation, all the terrible hazards he had faced in invading England, a land that could muster an army at least as efficient as his own and far stronger in numbers. He had circumvented the English fleet, landing without opposition. The weather had delayed his crossing, to his great advantage, as it turned out. Hardrada's fortuitous invasion had weakened Harold's army, and Harold, he calculated, would be tempted south by the wasting of his land and the murder of his people.

Harold should have taken Gyrth's advice. He should have refused William's battle, laying waste the countryside between London and the coast and denying the Normans supplies, while he collected an overwhelming force. William would then have had three choices. He could have stayed in Hastings, supplying his army from Normandy by his fleet, a poor prospect, as winter was setting in and the remobilized English fleet might sink his convoys and starve him out. He could go back to Normandy, a fearful risk as long as the English fleet patrolled the Channel and an admission of ignominious failure that would have made him the laughingstock of Europe. Or he could seek out Harold and fight him where he found him. Harold could ambush him in the Weald, the great forest between Hastings and London, or stand off, his army growing as William's wasted.

William took extraordinary risks in invading England. He could not count on the weather to help him, or on Hardrada to land at exactly the right moment. He calculated his risks on a slender thread, that Harold would act rashly, that he would hurry to fight the decisive battle. That was William's only chance of success. The much-vaunted Norman invasion of England, so long considered to have been a foregone conclusion, was in reality an audacious, rash enterprise, apparently destined for failure. It succeeded because the wind delayed William, because Harold was forced to fight a major battle in the North, and because he rushed to meet William with an inadequate force. Harold lost the Battle of Hastings because he was impetuous and perhaps unlucky. In the hundred years beginning with 1066, in which only six pitched battles were fought by Anglo-Norman armies, two were fought in England within twenty days of each other, and they were of longer duration and far heavier in casualties than the other four.*

During the six or seven days that Harold was in London, a great number of men answered his call to arms. The fyrd trickled slowly in from York. Still, a large part of his army was yet to come. Harold refused to delay longer. He made the fateful decision. On Thursday, 12 October, he left London with his housecarls, naming a rallying point

* Tinchebrai, 1106, Brèmule, 1119, Northalerton, 1138, Lincoln, 1141.

for the fyrd, on a spur of the Downs seven miles north of Hastings at the noted landmark, "The Place of the Hoar Apple Tree."

The bulk of the English army could have reached the trysting place by one of two routes: via the Lewes Way, turning off at Maresfield and marching through Netherfield, a distance of 61 miles from London, or more probably by following Watling Street as far as Rochester, from where an old Roman road ran south, via Cripps Corner, to Sedlescombe, from where a local track would have carried it to Caldbec Hill, on the slopes of which probably stood the Hoar Apple Tree. That way the distance from London would have been 64 miles. Support for the choice of this route for Harold's army is claimed from the find, in 1876, of a hoard of one thousand coins, bearing the effigy of Edward the Confessor, close to the road at Sedlescombe, still lying in a decayed box, perhaps an army treasure chest.

Ten

The Ridge

Harold reached the assembly point during the night of Friday the 13th or early next morning. William, the monk of Jumièges, says he rode all night. The army streamed in all night, weary and exhausted, and many of his troops were still arriving next day after the battle had been joined. *The Anglo-Saxon Chronicle* states that the battle commenced before they had all come, and William of Malmesbury says that Harold had few men with him. Florence of Worcester claims that half his army had not arrived by 9 A.M., and he says that there were many desertions up to the hour of the battle. According to Wace, the English spent the night before the battle laughing and drinking, gambling, dancing and singing, and Norman scouts overheard cries of "Bublie," "Weissel" and "Drincheleil." These calumnies were probably invented to emphasize the very different ways in which the Normans spent the night, in prayer and devotion. The English chroniclers agree, however, that the English were late in rousing next morning, not unlikely, for the men must have been tired after their forced march from London, more than sixty miles by road, and from elsewhere.

The events of the night and early morning are uncertain, for the chroniclers are imprecise and contradictory, and, in several instances, they may be repeating legends invented or exaggerated after the battle was decided. It is doubtful that Norman historians could have known what occurred in the English camp, far less the precise words of the secret deliberations of the English leaders, especially as there were few English survivors to repeat these conversations.

Wace relates that the English, fearing night attack, kept guard all night and that at break of day Harold and his brother Gyrth stole out of the camp, mounted their horses and went, unaccompanied by any guard, to reconnoiter the Norman camp. They examined the ground between the two armies and looked down from a hill upon the Norman host. They saw a great many huts made of branches of trees, tents, well-equipped pavilions and banners. They heard horses neighing and beheld the glitter of armor. They stood watching for a while without speaking. It is possible that, as Wace suggests, Harold and Gyrth went to spy on the Normans. They took great risk of capture, and their brother Leofwine was angry. He found the tent empty when he went to waken his brothers. Thinking the Normans had stolen into the camp and seized them, he roused the guards. Riding to the rescue, he met Harold and Gyrth returning, and "all took it ill that they had gone without a guard," records Wace. When the brothers regained their tent, there were angry words. Harold is made to appear timid. There are many good knights among the Normans, he says, and he asks Gyrth, "What do you advise?" telling him, "With so great a host against us, I dare not do otherwise than fall back on London; I will return thither and assemble a larger army." Gyrth replies that this counsel comes too late. The King would not listen when he had given him that advice in London. "If you turn back now," he warns, "everyone will say that you ran away," and he asks, "If men see you flee, who is to keep your men together?" If the army was allowed to disperse, it would never be brought together again.

This conversation is certainly mythical but, like the faintheartedness allegedly shown by Harold when the Normans appeared on the horizon, it may be based on truth. Harold's impetuous advance to give William battle near the coast was made against the advice of his brother and his other counsellors, and he may have regretted his hasty action when he saw for himself the Norman strength. Up to the moment of his early-morning reconnaissance, he knew the numbers and composition of the Norman army only by hearsay, from the reports of the thegn from Pevensey, the churl from Hastings and other refugees from Sussex, garbled accounts that he may have dismissed as wild exaggerations. Harold may have discounted stories of an immense host of horsemen, footmen and archers because he may have doubted that William could have transported so great a force over the sea.

Harold may have been fooled by William. Wace claims that when Harold saw the Normans deploying at the start of the battle, he said: "We are fallen on evil lot, and I fear much lest we come to shame. The Count of Flanders has betrayed me. I trusted to him, and was a fool for so doing; when he sent me word by letter, and assured me by messages, that William would never collect so great a chivalry, I delayed my preparations, and now I rue the delay." William, it seems, had used his father-in-law to beguile Harold into thinking that the Normans could muster only an inadequate force, as they would have done had William relied solely on his own barons and their men.

The Normans' feat in bringing their war-horses across the Channel must have astounded Harold. He had been a military and naval commander all his adult life; he was far more experienced at sea than was William. No nation in Western Europe, Harold knew, had succeeded in carrying, or had even tried to transport horses in ships. He knew from his own experiences in Brittany that the strength of the Norman army lay in its mounted knights. Without horses, they were of little account, and he did not expect them to bring horses to England, except possibly a few for the leaders to ride. His own mounted housecarls would be more than a match for dismounted Continental knights. He was astounded when he saw, on the morning of 14 October, that the Normans had many horses. The Duke had brought the armed knights of Northern France, hoping to conquer England. The danger was far more serious than Harold had feared. He may have regretted his impetuous dash to Sussex with a scratch force, and he may have considered a return to London, to await reinforcements before joining battle. Therein lay his dilemma. With great difficulty Harold had scraped together fresh levies, and many men of the fyrd were still on their way to the assembly point, badly strung out through the Weald. Their period of service was limited by the time for which they could be provisioned, and many of them had returned to their homes only a few weeks before, after their discouraging two months' wait on the south coast. Harold faced the terrible problem of medieval warfare: How long could he keep his army in being? If he abandoned his position and returned to London, he might find himself without an army. Harold rejected that course; he had planned originally to fight William, and fight him he would.

What exactly Harold proposed to do when he marched from London has been argued for centuries. Did he intend to assault the Normans in their camp, or did he intend to fight on the defensive, at a preselected spot, peculiarly suitable for static defense?

The great natural strength of the position where Harold ordered his army to assemble, and where he stood his ground, has been taken to prove that he always intended, having marched to meet William, to fight a defensive battle. There can be little question that Harold knew the place of the Hoar Apple Tree and had assessed its advantages for such an eventuality during his sojourn in Sussex during the summer, but he could not have counted, when he left London, on the Norman's sallying out of their entrenchments to attack him. During the two weeks he had been in England, William had made no move. He had missed the golden opportunity to advance on London while the English army was away in the North. Harold may have attributed the Duke's caution to lack of strength; William, he may well have believed, intended to await attack where he was protected by his ditches and palisades.

It is probable, and in keeping with his character, that Harold planned to march to Hastings and attack the Normans in their camp, or wherever he found them. Harold "wished to surprise and attack the duke" says William of Jumièges. He set out from London hoping to repeat the tactics that had gained his great victory over the Norsemen. He hoped partially to surprise William, who would not be expecting attack so soon after Harold's victory in the North, 260 miles away. William, Harold may have surmised, would not think it possible for him to assemble a fresh army so quickly. His sudden arrival near Hastings with an army would be unexpected. William might think it was no more than a reconnaissance in force. The royal housecarls, supported by the hurriedly raised levies, would be a sufficient force for him to crush William, who Harold believed had only a few horsemen with him. Harold's hopes of a quick victory were dashed when he saw the Norman host with his own eyes. He changed his plan. The appointed assembly place was ideally suited for defense. He decided to stand on the impregnable redoubt that nature had provided, the crest of the slope against which the Norman horsemen would dash themselves in vain.

We can assess the strength of the cross-ridge at Senlac, as one Norman chronicler subsequently named the site the Normans also called "Battle," as Harold saw it nine hundred years ago. The contours of the ground have changed little since then, but now buildings and trees obscure the scene of the great battle. The modern town and Battle Abbey cover much of the ground, the general level of which may have risen as much as nine feet since 1066.

Harold drew up his army on the cross-ridge forming the end of the spur of the downs that projected southward from the forest of Andredsweald. This spur, a narrow peninsula flanked by slopes and valleys, may be likened to a hammer, its shaft the peninsula, its head the cross-ridge. To appreciate the natural strength of the position the English occupied, it is best to explain it from north to south. About a mile to the north of the hammer's head, low hills rose from the forest to an altitude of three hundred feet, and through them ran two roads, one from the northwest and another from the northeast, by either of which Harold and the main part of his army may have come from London. The road to Robertsbridge, 25 miles directly to the north, did not then exist, except possibly as a local track. These roads converged just south of the highest point of the hills, Caldbec Hill, on the slopes of which may have stood the well-known landmark of the Hoar Apple Tree. The combined road, almost certainly an old Roman way, ran along the crest of the spur and crossed the ridge at its southern extremity. There it was bisected by an ancient east-west highway. The road ran down the southern slope of the ridge, through the valley below, and rose through the hills beyond toward Hastings, six miles away. Thus, apart from its natural features, the ridge at Senlac, as we may name it, was a focal point of roads, which made it an ideal assembly place for an army converging from several directions.

Let us imagine we are looking at an aerial photograph, from which all the modern buildings and trees have been removed. The ground on both sides of the spur, the hammer's shaft, sloped steeply down to boggy valleys, beyond which lay thickly wooded and marshy country. At the end of the spur, the ground broadened into the narrow cross-ridge, the hammer's head, below which it descended to a low, boggy valley.

The spur and its cross-ridge, it can thus be seen, were ideal positions for assembly and defense, for an army drawn up on the cross-ridge could not be outflanked or bypassed. It could be assaulted only from the front and sides, where it was protected by slopes of varying steepness. "It was admirably devised for infantry to resist cavalry," as Colonel Burne has remarked (*The Battlefields of England,* 1950).

The cross-ridge at the end of the spur faced almost squarely in the direction from which the Normans must advance if they took the offensive. It ran from east to southwest and, at its highest level, it extended for 800 to 1,000 yards. Its average height above sea level was 200–250 feet. At its highest point, just east of center, the crown of the ridge rose to 275 feet. It was bare of trees, and was dotted here and three, perhaps, by clumps of gorse and broom. Apart from its slopes, access to the ridge was made difficult by streams, eight arising around it. Two flowed in opposite directions, through the valley in front, making it boggy and swampy. Another rose at the eastern end of the valley, and several others rose and flowed beneath the western end of the ridge, where they had cut small, deep ravines.

The slopes of the ridge made assault by horsemen hard, and on the east virtually impossible, for there the fall at the back of the ridge was exceedingly steep, almost precipitous, the gradient in the rear being one in four, and at the side one in twelve. At the center of the ridge, where the road then dipped into the valley, the gradient averaged one in fifteen. The slopes at the western end were more gradual, about one in thirty-three. One other feature of the ground needs to be described. On the southern slope of the ridge, about 200 yards west of center, rose a low, detached hill, about 15 feet high, which stands to this day, and for convenience is called the "hillock." The valley south of the ridge was narrow on the east and wide on the west, the hills to the south rising steeply on the east and gradually on the west. The distance between the crest of the ridge and the equivalent contour on these hills was about one mile.

How Harold drew up his army on this ridge and the nature of the ground to the south, over which the Normans advanced from their camp at Hastings, will be discussed later. For the moment we can leave Harold, shortly after sunrise on the morning of Saturday, 14 October, considering how best to use the position nature had provided.

During the evening of 13 October, a trusty patrol of knights galloped into the Norman camp at Hastings. The English army was approaching, they informed William. This news must have been brought before dark, for the greater part of the Norman host, according to William of Poitiers, the Duke's chaplain, was out foraging. Fearing a night attack, William immediately recalled his men to camp.

His strategy had succeeded, William knew. He had enticed Harold to Sussex. As darkness fell, his knowledge was still scanty. An English army of unknown size was approaching. His retreat across the Channel was cut off by the English fleet, the seven hundred ships of which William may have seen patrolling the sea off Hastings. During the night William decided to march out of his camp and attack Harold next day. Because that is what he did, it is usually assumed that he always intended to do so. He may have been of two minds at first, whether to sally out of his entrenchments or to fight behind his ditches and barricades. The information, brought by scouts, that Harold's army was small and was strung out over a wide area may have decided his strategy. He may have known more than his scouts told him. His Norman friends in London could have told him of the inadequacy of the army Harold was assembling. William decided to attack Harold before his strength increased.

The Normans, and their French and Breton allies, spent the night in prayer and devotion, attending masses, which were celebrated by the two bishops, Eude of Bayeux, who extracted vows from the soldiers not to eat flesh again on a Saturday, the day of the battle, and Geoffrey Mowbray of Coutances. An altar, containing the bulk of the holy relics of Bayeux, was set up, at which the masses were said. The soldiers confessed their sins to priests, or, if there was not one available, accused themselves to their neighbors. The priests watched all night, says Wace, praying in their chapels, which they had set up throughout the host, crying to God for mercy, offering fasts, penances and orisons, so that the camp rang with the sound of psalms, hymns and paternosters.

At some time during the night or early morning, if we are to believe Wace, William sent an embassy to Harold, headed possibly by Hugh Margot, the monk of Fécamp, who may have spoken Anglo-Saxon. It is possible, even probable, that William made a last attempt to reach a peaceful settlement, in order to re-establish the fiction of his legal and rightful claim to the throne of England. He may have hoped also to spread fear and cause dissension among the English.

William's envoy offered Harold three choices: to resign England to the Duke and take the latter's daughter to wife, to submit to the judgment of the Pope (who had already decided in William's favor) or to meet William in single combat. This final alternative was a blind, to emphasize the personal nature of William's crusade and to show that he had come mainly to punish the perjurer and oathbreaker who had stolen the crown from him. If Harold would accept the first alternative, William offered him all England north of the Humber. His brother Gyrth was to have all the lands once owned by their father Godwine, and the English lords would keep their own lands. Harold and the men who supported him had been excommunicated by the Pope, said the envoy.

This untrue but nonetheless credible statement "much troubled" the English, who murmured that they wished the battle to be averted, states Wace. Gyrth addressed the doubters, warning them of William's treachery. If they accepted his offer, they would not long be left with their lands, for "he will push us out yet further and bring us to ruin in the end; when he has got the uppermost and has the best of the land, he will have little use for us and will soon get it all." William would cheat them. He had already given their lands to his knights and taken homage for their inheritances. The Normans would chase the English landlords away and kill them, pillage their vassals and ruin their sons and daughters. The Normans had not come for the good of the English lords but for their ruin, Gyrth reminded his friends, stressing that Harold had never taken or given away their lands. "If you lose your lands, what will become of you, whither will you and your families flee?" he asked. "You will go a-begging." Gyrth's counsel prevailed. Thus aroused, says Wace, the English magnates were eager to fight, especially those who had previously cried for peace. When the messenger returned to William, the latter made no further attempt to negotiate. He called his men to arms.

Dawn broke on the morning of Saturday, 14 October, the day of Saint Calixtus, about 5:30 A.M., and the sun rose at 6:20 A.M. A two-thirds waning moon, still high in the sky at dawn, illuminated the morning, which was unusually light for the season, the chroniclers remark. In the Norman camp, the soldiers were busy, straightening lances, fitting hauberks and helmets, making ready saddles and stirrups, filling quivers, stringing bows and generally preparing for battle, a scene that may have been watched by English spies. Observing so many shaven men, they reported to Harold that the Normans were all priests and mass-sayers. Laughing at their mistake, the King told them, "They are valiant knights, bold and brave warriors, though they do not wear beards and moustaches as we do."

The Normans must have marched from their camp before 6 A.M., perhaps even earlier. The Tapestry depicts the barons and knights riding out dressed for battle, but *The Chronicle of Battle Abbey,* which is supported by Wace, says they did not don their armor until later, which is more probable as the heavy mail shirts were fatiguing to wear and were not usually put on until battle was imminent.

The column, which must have been at least three miles in length, marched northward from Hastings along the saddle of the narrow ridge, on which the Normans were protected from flank attack by steep hillsides clothed with woods. The army marched quickly over the level ground until its head, at which rode William, reached a hill named "Hechelande" in *The Chronicle of Battle Abbey*. This hill, which was also for many centuries appropriately named "Standard Hill," has been identified by Mr. F. H. Baring, from examination of the Abbey's records, as the modern Blackhorse Hill, the highest point on the road between Hastings and Battle. It rises to an altitude of 462 feet and is situated almost exactly two miles from the cross-ridge at Senlac, which, however, cannot be seen from that point, as the Tapestry confirms, for it shows William sending scouts ahead to reconnoiter while he calls a halt for his army to assemble.

As the soldiers, or some of them, come up, William harangues them, delivering a prebattle pep talk, in which he reminds them of the great victories the Normans have won under his leadership. William of Poitiers, who may have been present, records the gist of the Duke's speech:

> Now is the time for you to show your strength, and the courage that is yours. You fight not merely for victory but also for survival. If you bear yourselves valiantly, you will obtain victory, honour and riches. If not, you will be ruthlessly butchered, or else led ignominiously captive into the hands of pitiless enemies. Further, you will incur abiding disgrace. There is no room for retreat. In front, your

> advance is blocked by an army, and a hostile countryside; behind you, there is the sea where an enemy fleet bars your flight. Men worthy of the name do not allow themselves to be dismayed by the number of their foes. The English have again and again fallen to the sword of an enemy; often, being vanquished, they have submitted to a foreign foe; nor have they ever been famed as soldiers. The vigorous charge of a few men armed in a just cause and specially protected by Heaven must prevail against a host of men unskilled in combat. Only be bold so that nothing shall make you yield, and victory shall be yours.

"Sire, we tarry too long, let us arm ourselves. Allons, Allons," cries William Fitz-Osbern, as the Duke finishes. Some knights, already equipped for battle, press forward, one horseman alone turning his head to catch William's concluding words. The rest of the knights and barons arm themselves. The Duke calls for his hauberk. When his esquire brings it, William, turning it inadvertently, puts it over his head back to front. He changes it quickly but not before those who watched cry that the mistake is an ill omen. Though he dislikes diviners and prophets, William is never loath to turn superstition to good account. The hauberk that was turned wrong and then set right signifies a change, he explains. "A king shall I be, who hitherto have been but a duke," he tells the onlookers. Girding on his sword, William mounts the war-horse sent by the King of Spain, ordering that three spare horses be equipped for him. He completes his arming by hanging round his neck the choicest relics of Bayeux, the saintly bones over which Harold had sworn his fatal oath.

The sight of the noble Duke, sitting astride his war-horse, dressed for battle, was too much for one of his followers, the Viscount of Tours, who cried out: "Never have I seen a man so fairly armed, nor one who rode so gallantly, or bore his arms, or became a hauberk, so well; neither anyone who bore his lance so gracefully, or sat his horse and manoeuvered him so nobly. There is no such knight under Heaven. A fair count he is, and a fair king he will be."

The Bayeux Tapestry shows William at this stage of the march, seated on his horse and holding a heavy mace in his right hand. The Duke is represented as being of no greater stature than the men around him, a circumstance that belies the legend of his great size, a view which is expressed by the many contemporary references to *Willelmus Magnus*. The great Duke was, we know now, of quite moderate height by present-day standards. When his tomb at Saint Stephen's in Caen was opened for the first time in 1522, the stone coffin revealed the body of a large man, with unusually long legs and arms. The tomb was desecrated in the next century by Calvinists, who destroyed all but one bone, a single femur, which, when measured, indicated a man of only about 5 feet 10 inches in height. Nonetheless, other evidence suggests that William was burly in build. A painting was made from his body when the tomb was opened in 1522. It did not survive, but there is a picture painted in the eighteenth century that may be a copy of it. The later picture shows that William was a massive man, fleshy-faced and with russet red hair, a representation that confirms the words of the monk of Caen, who may have seen William in life and who describes him as a burly warrior, great in stature but not ungainly.

The halt at Hechelande is terminated by an incident that the Tapestry records. A scout named Vital, who appears to be the chief of a troop of horsemen sent ahead to reconnoiter, perhaps the same man named in Domesday as a follower of the Bishop of Bayeux, returns to report. He points eagerly in the direction of the brow of a wooded eminence where his men are hiding, one of them standing with his hand shading his eyes. In reply to the Duke's inquiry about the position of the English, Vital tells him that King Harold stands among the thick ranks of men that crown the summit of a hill, for there he has seen the royal standard. William knows now that he has brought Harold to battle. He vows that, if God will give him the victory over his perjured foe, he will raise a mighty minster to His honor on the spot where the royal standard stands. His words are overheard by a monk from the Abbey of Marmoutier near Tours, William Faber by name, who secures the Duke's promise to dedicate the establishment to his abbey's patron, St. Martin, the soldier-saint of Normandy.

William orders his standard to be raised. A serving man brings the papal banner, the consecrated emblem of the great crusade against England. He unfurls and rears it. The Duke calls to Raoul de Conces, the hereditary standard-bearer of Normandy. "Bear my gonfalon, for I would but do you right," he tells him. Raoul begs to be quit of the honor. He wishes to fight in the battle. William turns to the aged Walter Giffard, his old friend and faithful retainer. "Do you take this gonfalon and bear it in battle," he orders. Giffard, too, asks to be excused the honor. "For God's mercy, Sire, look at my white and bald head," he pleads. His strength has fallen away and his breath has become short, he says. He will fight in the battle and strike with his sword until it is dyed with the blood of the Duke's enemies. The standard, he suggests, should be borne by someone who can better endure the long labor. Fierce anger sweeps the Duke. "My lords, I think you mean to betray me, and fail me in my hour of need," he exclaims, his eyes flashing. "We have done no treason," Giffard assures the Duke. He has a duty to lead a great diversity of soldiers, both mercenaries and the men of his own fief. Never has he had such good means of serving his lord as now. The Duke's anger evaporates as quickly as it arose. "By my faith," he replies "I have always loved you, and now I love you more." If they both survive the day, his old friend will be the better for it all his days, he assures Walter Giffard.

The Duke gave the consecrated banner to the care of another knight, named Tosteny, who took it gratefully and bore it gallantly. His services were not forgotten by William. He gave Tosteny's heirs quittance of the service they owed, and he promised that they should hold their lands forever. In after years, the family in Normandy, in memory of the great office held by its ancestor at the Battle of Hastings, took for supporters of their arms two angels, each bearing a banner.

William ordered the advance and the army moved forward in full battle array. It mounted the rise at Blackhorse Hill and poured down the slopes of Telham Hill, spreading out as the ground widened and fell away. William rode at the head of his men, Tosteny by his side, the great barons of Normandy and the leaders of the volunteer contingents and mercenary soldiers clustered about them. The spot from where William caught his first glimpse of the English army on the ridge opposite is not easy to identify. He could have seen the crest at a distance of 800 yards, from a place on the slopes of Telham Hill, on the 300 foot contour, about ¾ of a mile west of the road. From there only, could he have looked over the shoulder of the hill and the two intervening spurs, as I, myself, observed in 1964. In front of him, the ground fell gradually to the west and more steeply to the east. If William kept to the road, he would have had to advance to within 400 yards of the English before he could see them, an unlikely contingency, for he needed to oversee the battleground before deploying his men. He had probably seen the place before, on one of his reconnaissance expeditions from Hastings.

When the Norman host appeared over Telham Hill, Harold, according to *The Anglo-Saxon Chronicle,* was taken by surprise. The Normans came upon him "unexpectedly" before his army was set in order, a likely possibility, for he may not have expected the Normans to arrive so quickly, after their six-mile march from Hastings.

Harold sees the Normans, afar off, advancing over the rising ground. The first division marches down the hill. Harold spots the Duke, recognizable even at that distance by the pennons of the barons who surround him and by the Papal gonfalon borne at his side. "Brother, where are you looking? See the Duke coming yonder?" Harold calls to Gyrth. The sight of the advancing army has calmed his fears. "Our people will have no mischief from the force I see yonder. These are not men enough to conquer the great force we have in this land," he cries exultantly. Gyrth is more realistic. "You have many men," he tells his brother, "but a great force of villagers is worth little in battle," he warns. "You have plenty of men in everyday clothes," he says. The Normans, however, he goes on, are men to be feared, well armed and equipped, and they are mounted on horses which will trample Harold's army underfoot.

"Be not dismayed," Harold bids his gloomy brother. "There is certainly no need to be alarmed at yonder army," he remarks. While he speaks, another Norman division, larger than the first, comes into view. Now its size dismays Harold. "See how our enemies grow," he exclaims. "I fear the result of the battle, and my heart is in great tribulation," he groans. "You should have stayed in London; you did ill to fix a day for battle," answers Gyrth. The king had rejected his advice; it is too late now to follow it. They must defend themselves as best they can; there is no other remedy. "I did it for good," says Harold. He had chosen to fight on a Saturday, for that is his lucky day. "You were born on a Saturday and on that day also you may be killed," mocks Gyrth, turning aside to watch the arrival of still another division. As the brothers watch, the Normans stream down the opposite slope.

Whatever was the quality of the English army at the Battle of Hastings, Harold had no reason to be frightened by the size of the Norman host. He stood in a strong position, an impregnable redoubt, as long as his men held their ground on the ridge. His famed housecarls, though thinned in ranks, were a match for the cavalry of Normandy. The bulk of his troops, the scrapings of the countryside no doubt, men called together from the villages and bearing such arms as they could find—clubs and great picks, iron forks and stakes—were sturdy fighters, stirred by patriotism, many of them local Sussex men, eager to avenge the despoliation of their land and their homes. "All who could bear arms, and who had learned the news of the duke's arrival, came to defend the land," records Wace. But there was one great imponderable factor; would the men of the fyrd obey the strict orders Harold had given that morning?

When scouts brought tidings of the approach of the Normans, Harold called his men to battle, riding round their ranks to give his last orders in person. They were to keep together and to defend themselves as a body, he commanded. No man was to move from where he stood; each man was to defend his own place. The Normans, he said, were valiant knights, well used to battle. "All is lost if they once penetrate our ranks," he warned his soldiers. "Stand firm and cleave wherever you can, and spare naught," he urged them.

When he saw that all was ready, the King rode to the crown of the ridge and dismounted by his standard, the golden dragon of Wessex. By his side, a retainer bore his own banner, the emblem of the fighting man, wrought in gold. Around him many earls and thegns grouped themselves. The English closed their ranks. They stood on the ridge ready for battle, eager for the fight, ranged with their faces turned toward the foe, shouting their war cries, *Olicrosse, Godsmite.* From the opposite slope echoed the Norman reply, *Dex Aie, God's Aid.*

The English army was invincible, as long as it held its position. Along the crest of the ridge stretched the close array, the phalanx of axemen and spearmen, the famed Anglo-Saxon shield wall. In front the slopes fell into the valley; treacherous boggy ground, difficult for horsemen. William had brought Harold to battle. But Harold stood on ground of his own choosing.

Eleven

The Shield Wall

The two armies come into each other's sight. The Normans and their allies move down the slopes of Telham Hill, advancing in three great divisions, two spreading to the right and left, the third holding its center course, all rolling downhill, their thick ranks taking the shape of a gigantic three-pronged fork. At sight of their enemy, the English, a full 400 yards away, instinctively clutch their weapons, lifting their shields, raising their spears and axes. A ripple of movement runs through the ranks. Across the valley, the Duke's soldiers eye the men they have come to dispossess, despoil and punish. They see a forest of spears, their steel-clad tips shimmering and glinting in the sunshine of the bright morning, beneath them a compact wedge of men.

Duke William gives his order. From his place on the slopes several riders, their horses' hooves thundering on the turf, gallop to the three divisions, slowly uncoiling from the column of march. The bearers of the Duke's order reach the army's captains. "Deploy, deploy," they cry. "Form line of battle," they command. A tumult breaks out. Trumpets blare, bugles call; the thin piping notes of horns add to the din. Officers shout, sergeants bellow, horses neigh. The divisions billow and swirl, their footmen, archers and horsemen turning and pressing to the front. The three prongs of the fork merge into a triple line of men. From across the valley, it seems that three enormous snakes are casting their skins.

William watches the deployment from his command post, a spot just west of the road from Hastings where it dips into the valley below, somewhere near, it is thought, the old tannery (replaced now by a garage), a position from which the Duke can give orders by both hand and mouth. The army extends in open order, moving down into the valley. Its divisions are arranged according to the geographical distribution of the men's places of origin, an arrangement allowing neighbor to fight alongside neighbor, under the eyes of his friends.

At the right of the road march the volunteers from France, from Flanders, Picardy and Boulogne, and with them the mercenary soldiers from many lands, the men who fight for gain. "Go and take command of the right wing," William orders Roger de Montgomery. "I rely on you to lead your men to attack the English on that side," he tells him. "William Fitz-Osbern shall go with you," he commands, waving to his seneschal. The two barons ride to lead the first division, conspicuous among whose banners and flags are the pennons of Eustace of Boulogne and young Roger Beaumont, whose first battle this is.

Command of the third division, in which ride the Bretons, the Angevins, the Poitevins and the barons from Maine and their companies, destined to assault the ridge from the left, is given to Alan Fergant, the Duke's son-in-law, a cousin of the reigning Count of Brittany.

"I will lead my own men, my friends and my own kindred, in the middle throng where the battle will be thickest," announces William. Surrounded by his great barons, the friends of his youth, the men who had prospered with him, William leads his Norman knights into the center of the host. Beside him ride his two half-brothers, Robert, Count of Mortain, and Eude, Bishop of Bayeux, the warrior-prelate who salves his conscience by carrying a heavy iron mace so as not to incur the displeasure of his church by actually shedding blood. With the Duke also are his friends and staunch supporters, William Giffard, Roger Bigod, William Paltry and William Malet. At the left of the Duke's division rides his old enemy, the one-time rebel, Neil of Saint Sauveur, commanding the knights from the Cotentin. On the slopes above congregated "the youths and common herd of the camp," whose business was not to join in the battle, reports Wace. The priests and clerks, he says, also stayed on the hill, there to offer up prayers to God and watch the battle.

The slopes of Telham, the ridge at Senlac and the valley between, which once rang with the clash of arms and the shouts and cries of men bent on victory or death, are now quiet and peaceful. A group of horses cluster around the ponds and streams; a herd of cows crop the lush grass in the valley, through which runs the road from Battle to Bexhill. The famous "hillock" rises on the slope to the ridge, the ground around it still treacherous and boggy. The stillness of the old battlefield is deceptive; the Battle of Hastings is still being fought by historians and military commentators. Unlike the Normans and the English, we cannot plunge straight into the fray. Several problems require discussion before we can understand what happened.

Where on the ridge did Harold draw up his line of battle? Clearly, the length of the English line was conditioned by the number of men available and by their quality as soldiers. Harold's army numbered, the evidence suggests, about seven to eight thousand men, for Wace reports that the Normans were not more numerous than the English, and the invaders' effective strength seems to have been about 7,500 men of all types. We may dismiss as wild exaggeration the statement of William of Poitiers that, at the passage of Harold's host, "the rivers became dry and the forests were turned into plains." Harold, we may deduce from the scanty information available, had three types of soldiers; the royal bodyguard, the famed housecarls, their strength reduced to perhaps 2,000 men; those members of the select fyrd of the South who had returned from the North and the fyrdworthy men whom Harold had recruited on his march from York, another 2,000 men, perhaps; and a mass of peasants, the great fyrd of Sussex and Kent, who may have numbered 3,500 ill-armed rustics.

Harold had to choose his position both with regard to the number and effectiveness of his men and with an eye to the ground. Here the Tapestry helps us, for its pictures show that the English front line was composed of soldiers, armored and armed in the same fashion as the Norman knights, which identifies them as the housecarls. It seems probable, considering the type of attack he was expecting, that Harold placed most of his well-armed professional soldiers in the front of the shield wall, or "war hedge," as the Saxons called it, massing the lightly armed, part-time soldiers and rustics of the fyrd behind the first phalanx of axes and spears. He may have kept about five hundred housecarls in reserve, grouped around his standard.

Thus, if Harold had 1,500 housecarls available for his front line, we can roughly assess the probable length of the shield wall, a term of which we need to be wary, for it conjures up a false conception of a long line of shields, touching or even interlocking, either of which would have given the spearmen, and particularly the axemen, insufficient room to thrust and swing their weapons. The kite-shaped shields used by the housecarls, with a few exceptions, and by the Norman knights, measured, as church effigies show, fifteen and one-half inches in width, and the Englishmen would still have had small freedom of movement if they had stood "shoulder to shoulder," or twenty inches apart. It seems more likely that each man occupied two feet of ground, which would have made the maximum length of the line one thousand yards.

The natural features of the ground, which are still evident once allowance has been made for the buildings by which it is partially covered, suggest that the English line extended for not more than 800 yards, perhaps even less, an estimate apparently supported by the description of William of Poitiers, who says that the English stood in a "closely gathered ring." Again we need to be careful, for the term "ring," which he may have employed to lend picturesque detail to his narrative, suggests that the English shield wall curved back upon itself, as had the Norse line at Stamford Bridge, according to Snorri. At Senlac the English would have been better served by a straight line of soldiers, with their flanks thrown slightly back, than by a ring of men encircling the ridge's crown, which would have lost to them the advantage of the steeply sloping banks at the rear ends of the ridge.

A straight line of under 800 yards in length approximates closely the best defensive qualities of the ridge, if it was manned by the number of men estimated. Fortunately, in determining the line's location, we have one fixed point to guide us, for Harold's command point is almost exactly pinpointed by the foundations of the Abbey's chapel, the high altar of which was built on the spot where he fought and fell. The English King, we are told, raised his standard on the "very crown of the ridge," which rose then about 25 feet above the 250-foot contour at the intersection of the east-west highway with the main road to the coast, which crossed the saddle of the ridge at that point. It runs now, it needs to be explained, farther to the east, for the building of the Abbey necessitated that the ancient road be diverted. Its original course can still be determined from the farm track that climbs the slope from the floor of the valley and disappears at the top of the slope. Its imaginary extension runs through the chapel and joins the main road beyond, making a straight line, whereas the present road is artificially curved.

Harold could have looked from his command post over the heads of his men, who were ranged below him and, it seems probable, along the crest of the ridge 375 yards to his east and 425 yards to the west of him. The position of the English left flank is easier to determine than the end of the right flank, for the nature of the ground provides a likely fixed point for its termination. Harold needed to find protection for his flanks, for he knew he would be assailed by horsemen who had to be prevented from overlapping and riding round the ends of the shield wall. We may imagine him, early in the morning, followed by his earls and thegns, riding along the level ridge, inspecting the ground and casting anxious glances to the south, the direction from which the Normans would come.

The ridge sloped gently down toward the west and gradually to the east, where about 400 to 600 yards from the crown, it fell precipitately toward the rear. At the back the bank was more than 50 feet high and steep enough to give complete protection to a flank thrown back upon it at an angle. Harold's alternative choice would have been to extend the line for a further 200 to 400 yards, where he would have lost the advantage of the protection afforded his rear and risked attack up the comparatively easy slope from the southeast, where the end of the ridge broadened and fell gently into the valley below. His left flank would have been weaker at 800 yards than at 400 yards. At the shorter distance he could have anchored it on the bank along the line of the 250-foot contour on the Wasingate Highway, somewhere near the present intersection of Battle High Street and Marley Lane, near the state school.

Where the English right flank terminated can never be determined exactly. The natural features of the ground suggest a point about 425 yards west of the crown, on the 250-foot contour. The ridge narrowed at a distance of 400 to 800 yards, and at 400 yards its rear is protected by the Asten Stream, the 20 foot bank of which was steep enough to deter horsemen attacking from the rear. Point 425 yards west was not the end of the ridge, but it occupied higher ground, and provided protection to a flank curved slightly to the northwest. If Harold had mustered more men than we think, his right flank could have been farther to the west.

With his flanks secured, Harold could extend his men over a distance of 800 yards. In the rear were massed the men of the fyrd, so crowded together on the western end of the ridge that many were forced to withdraw to the spur at the back, congested, we may assume, with camp-followers and the tethered horses of the earls, thegns and housecarls. The militia may have been grouped in ten or twelve ranks. In front stood the housecarls, drawn up in a fairly straight line, their shields close but not touching. Ahead, the ground sloped gradually to the floor of the boggy valley, dropping about 50 feet on the left and more gently on the right. Nowhere was the ascent steep. Out in front of the line, about 200 to 300 yards west of the center, rose the small hillock, a forward position which the English may have occupied at the start of the battle, a place which was to take on a sinister significance later.

On the crest of the ridge stood a wall of flesh and blood. Harold had sufficient warning of the Norman approach to draw up his men, many of whom had only arrived during the night and were still streaming in to the assembly point, well-authenticated facts that disprove the once-held belief that the English dug a ditch and built a palisade along their front. This theory was developed in the nineteenth century by Professor Freeman and was ridiculed by Professor Round in a controversy that the latter joyfully described as "the fiercest of the generation." Freeman based his belief in an artificial breastwork on the description by Henry of Huntingdon, who speaks of a *quasi castellum,* and on the words of Wace, who relates:

> . . . the English peasants carried hatchets, and keen-edged bills. They had built up a fence before them with their shields, and with ash and other wood; and had well-joined and wattled in the whole work, so as not to leave even a crevice; and thus they had a barricade in their front, through which any Norman who attacked them must pass.

Wace, it is thought, may have been misled by the Anglo-Saxon term "shield wall," or "war hedge," which he conceived as a threefold palisade, defended by an artificial ditch. On the other hand, he may have heard a traditional story that the ridge was the site of a battle between King Alfred and the Danes in 893–894, at which banks and ditches were thrown up. Whatever was the source of his belief, it is improbable that the exhausted English soldiers would have had time to construct such a massive defensive work, of whose existence the other chroniclers and the Bayeux Tapestry give no hint.

This picture of the English army, dismounted and drawn up on foot, as William of Poitiers confirms, raises the question, if the English could mount cavalry assaults in one battle, why were they rooted to the ground in another? The answer is both simple and complicated.

Conditions at Stamford Bridge and at Hastings were different. In Yorkshire, Harold was the aggressor, advancing over a flat plain suitable for horsemen. In Sussex, circumstances forced him to stand on the defensive, at a spot peculiarly suitable for defense behind the traditional Anglo-Saxon shield wall. Much as he would have liked, no doubt, to have kept his mounted housecarls in reserve, poised to launch a counterattack, the poor quality of his rustic army demanded that he dismount his professional soldiers to stiffen the ranks of the militia. Because Harold did that, when any other tactic would have been madness, it is claimed that the English always fought on foot and that they were no match for mounted Continental knights. On the contrary, it may be argued that the dismounted housecarls, backed by the fyrd, if they had not been forced to fight a major battle two weeks before, would have been more than a match for javelin-throwing horsemen, which is what eleventh-century mounted soldiers were. These horsemen were called *miles* and *chevallers* by the Normans and *knights* by the English. The Anglo-Saxon word stuck, and it has created an image that gives a misleading picture of eleventh-century warfare.

The true knight, the thirteenth-century paladin, the plate-armored, faceless horseman mounted on an equally well-protected horse, symbol of aristocratic wealth and power, charged knee to knee, with lance couched, galloping in a thundering unwavering wall of steel-clad men and horses, and crashed through the enemy lines by force of impact. Such shock tactics were possible because the knights were similarly armed, because they were trained to act in concert in regular formation and, above all, because the horses were armored.

The horse soldier of the eleventh century had not reached that advanced stage of military development. Compared to the tank of 1917 and the panzer of 1940, he was no more than an armored man on a bicycle. He wore a long shirt of chain mail, reaching to below the knee, and a hauberk, which protected the neck and throat. In the twelfth century, it became attached to the shirt, the whole of which, in consequence, being named the "hauberk." A conical iron cap furnished with a "nasal" protected the face. A blunt pointed two-edged cutting sword was slung at his side, and he carried light lances and javelins. He rode up to the line of enemy foot soldiers, threw his javelins and turned away, repeating the maneuver until he and his companions had breached a gap through which they rode, cutting and hacking right and left, hoping to widen the breach. He may have occasionally thrust and prodded with his lance, but he did not charge the bristling line of spears and axes, for the simple reason that his horse would have "refused," as it is termed, and shied away. Against well-armed and disciplined troops, the javelin-throwing horseman was ineffective, as the Battle of Hastings proved. He was an efficient, indeed an essential factor in warfare, when horsemen fought against horsemen as, for example, at Val-ès-Dunes. Even then, each horseman fought personal encounters; there was no concerted action, although the barons and their tenants developed some esprit-de-corps from the intimate character of their relationship. It is thus quite incorrect to say, as Sir Charles Oman has said,* that the horsemen who fought at Hastings were "the now fully-developed cavalry of feudalism."

Eleventh-century horsemen constituted only a slight evolution from the light-armed cavalry which had for centuries accompanied Asiatic armies and had been adopted by the Romans for skirmishing and for the pursuit of a beaten army. But, since the days of Alexander and Hannibal, one tremendous revolution had occurred; the stirrup was introduced into Europe about the sixth century. It seated the rider firmly in the saddle and enabled him to rise and deliver an effective blow or thrust without falling or being pushed off his horse. The control stirrups enabled the individual rider to move with others in concerted

* See *The Art of War in the Middle Ages,* 1924.

action, a maneuver which took hundreds of years to perfect, by which time the weapons of defense had caught up with the new tactic and the principle had become firmly established that cavalry should never charge unbroken infantry.

The Bayeux Tapestry is an unique record of warfare contemporary with its design. It shows how the Normans and English fought at Hastings and the weapons they used. Its pictures were stitched within twenty years of the battle, at the order of Bishop Eude, who fought at Hastings. He lived to see the Tapestry hung in his own cathedral, to fit the nave for which it was designed. Let us see what its amazing detail tells us.

The Norman horsemen rode to the attack, bearing kite-shaped shields and carrying slender, light lances, a few bearing pennons, which, says Wace, enabled the soldiers with similar devices painted on their shields, to recognize their friends and avoid killing one another. These devices were not yet personal heraldic bearings but were rather the emblems of sections and troops. At the start of the battle, the horsemen were preceded by archers, only a few of whom were dressed in armor. The others wore leather jerkins. None were crossbowmen, whom, it is assumed, William of Poitiers and Guy of Amiens later introduced into the story of the battle under the name "balistanes." The true crossbow was a later invention, and it is not mentioned in literature until 1098, by William of Tyre. It had, however, a parent, the "balista," a magnified crossbow, which had been in use since 537, for one of these missile-throwing engines was used by Belisarius to defend the walls of Rome. Procopius (*De Bell. Gott.* I, 21) describes it:

> These machines have the general shape of a bow, but in the middle there is a hollow piece of horn loosely affixed to the bow, and lying over a straight iron stock. When wishing to let fly at the enemy you pull back the short cord which joins the arms of the bow, and place in the horn a bolt, four times as thick as an ordinary arrow, but only half its length. The bolt is not feathered like an arrow, but furnished with wooden projections exactly reproducing the shape of the feathers. Men standing on each side of the balista draw back the cord with little devices; when they let it go, the horn rushes forward and discharges the bolt, which strikes with a force equal to at least two arrows, for it breaks stone and pierces trees.

The Normans, it seems, used this weapon, which was wound up with a winch and discharged bolts, we know from Procopius' account, sufficiently powerful, if well directed, to nail a man to a tree. It could also fire javelins. Within thirty years of the Battle of Hastings, some unknown genius, as Sir Charles Oman observes, conceived the idea of making a small hand-balista, which could be carried and worked by a single soldier, a notable contribution to the art of war.

The Norman "knights," if we may so call them, according to the Tapestry, rode up to the shield wall in disorderly groups. There was no uniformity of armament, as would be required for a concerted charge. Some carried swords, some maces, some spears. They threw their lances overhand, and we see the missiles in flight or piercing the bodies of the enemy. A few used their lances as stabbing weapons from a distance, but throwing was the rule, thrusting the exception. They made no attempt to break the English line otherwise than by missile attack. Only one Englishman is shown being ridden down. The horsemen acted as javeliners, and they were not loath to discard their horses and fight on foot. They used their two-edged swords only at close quarters, always cutting, never stabbing.

It is significant that the Norman tactics required from the English none of the thirteenth-century methods for repulsing cavalry, no bristling hedge of stoutly held pikes, against which the horses would refuse to charge home. The English soldiers repelled the attacks by casting their spears and by braining with their axes the horses that come too close. The weapons on each side, except the axes, were identical and interchangeable. It is one of the oldest rules of war, remarks Mr. Warren Hollister, that weapons dictate tactics. Neither the Normans or the English were equipped to make or receive cavalry charges. This does not prove, however, that the Norse army at Stamford Bridge was not so prepared, for, points out Mr. Hollister, there were many Flemings among Tostig's men, and they may have been the first people in Europe to use long pikes with which to resist cavalry, even before the year 1100. Snorri, we recall, refers to Hardrada's ordering the first line of his men to place the butts of their lances on the ground and the second line to point their lances at the horses' breasts. His statement is either an anachronism or the earliest known reference to the tactic that eventually stopped the charging knight.

The Tapestry shows that the English front line was composed of the housecarls who, except for the five-foot, double-edged axe, which was introduced into England by the Danes, were armored and armed identically with the Norman horsemen, though a few carried the obsolescent round shield, with which they may have re-equipped themselves after their own had been damaged at Stamford Bridge. The solitary English archer was identical with his leather-jerkined Norman counterpart. The English are depicted as larger even than the Normans, and they are identified by their moustaches. The housecarls wear the long byrne, the leather tunic on which are riveted thousands of separately forged iron rings, and a conical helmet with a nasal. The spearmen cast their lances and the axemen throw their small axes before swinging their terrible two-handed weapons, which can slice through man and beast at close quarters. Shields are used only for protection against missiles. The men of the fyrd wear no armor, and they carry swords and spears. To resist assault by horsemen, the English line has one serious defect; we note the absence of the archers, who had shot with such deadly effect at Stamford Bridge and who were probably still on their way from York. Their bows, the short variety, for the English longbow is still a weapon of the future, might have been enough to stop the Norman horsemen one hundred yards short of the shield wall.

The battlefield of Hastings presents several other problems, some of which can be dealt with as they arise. At what stages certain incidents of the battle occurred must remain uncertain, for the authorities are contradictory. It seems probable, for example, that Gyrth and his brother Leofwine were killed late rather than early, for the former appears to have been slain by Duke William, who does not seem to have been engaged personally in the early stages of the battle. The Tapestry and the chronicle of William of Poitiers are the principal authorities for the battle. William had been a soldier before becoming a priest, and he accompanied the invaders as the Duke's Chaplain. Though his narrative does not suggest that he was an eyewitness to the battle, he would have had the advantage of firsthand information within a few hours of its decision. The value of the other authorities is discussed in Appendix C. A word of warning: The chroniclers employ the titles "the Normans" and "the Frenchmen," indiscriminately when they mean the Norman host.

The name *Senlac* for the battle presents another vexing problem, for which there is no final solution. It was used first by Ordericus Vitalis in the twelfth century, apparently as the French equivalent of the Anglo-Saxon word *Sandlache,* meaning a sandy stream; probably the name of a watercourse near the English position, for the word *Sandlake* survived until 1250 as the name of a tithing in the borough of Battle and as the name of several village streets until modern times. The later French word *senguelac,* or *blood lake,* appears to have been a grim pun on the original name. Domesday Book calls the battle "Hastings," and the battle is referred to in other documents as having occurred *in planis Hastinges,* in the open country near the town.

We left the Normans and their allies streaming down the slopes of Telham Hill, descending into the valley in front of the English position, deploying in three divisions under the eyes of the Duke. To him comes a minstrel named Taillefer, for whose exploit at the start of the battle there seems reasonable evidence, for it is recorded by Wace and by Guy of Amiens in *De Bello Hastingensis Carmen*. Taillefer, who, in the words of Wace, "sang right well," rode before the Duke on a swift horse, singing of Charlemagne and Roland, of Oliver and his vassals at Roncevalles, by which Wacc, it is thought, may have meant, not the famous Roland, but rather the Duke's ancestor, Rollo, or even his father, Rognavald.

"A boon, Sire," asks Taillefer, drawing close to the Duke. "I have long served you, and you owe me for all such service," he tells him. "To-day, so please you, you shall repay it. I ask as my guerdon, and I beseech you for it earnestly, that you will allow me to strike first blow in the battle." "I grant it," replies the Duke. Wace recounts the incident, as he heard the story, omitting the detail added by other chroniclers, that Taillefer rode toward the English line juggling with his lance, which he hurled into the air and caught by its point.

> Then Taillefer put his horse to a gallop, charging before all the rest, and struck an Englishman dead, driving his lance below the breast into his body, and stretching him upon the ground. Then he drew his sword and struck another, crying out "Come on. Come on. What do ye, sirs, lay on. Lay on." At the second blow he struck, the English pushed forward and surrounded him.

Wace passes over Taillefer's inevitable fate and his story of knight-errantry poses several difficulties, for the Englishmen with whom Taillefer fought were apparently outside the shield wall, which suggests that they were either skirmishers or men who sallied out to meet the lone horseman.

The battle began in earnest shortly after 9 A.M., a time recorded by several chroniclers. The three divisions of the host, the French on the right, the Normans in the center and the Bretons on the left, advanced in good order across the floor of the valley, grouped according to the Duke's orders. In the van of each, according to William of Poitiers, the Duke had placed foot soldiers, equipped with bows and crossbows (by which he probably meant "slings"); in the second rank came the more heavily armed infantry, wearing hauberks, and behind them trotted squadrons of knights, in the midst of whom rode the Duke himself, showing invincible courage, we are told. The Tapestry, on the other hand, ignores the presence of infantry, other than archers, in the battle, the start of which was signalled by the terrible sound of trumpets. In the Tapestry, the horsemen are preceded by archers, whose clouds of hissing arrows, shot from below, are caught on the English shields. The first attempt to soften up the English line proved ineffective, and a wave of infantry was sent charging up the slope. It reeled back from the shield wall, which presented its solid front, unimpaired by the assault.

Twelve

The Knights

Duke William throws in his horsemen, his mounted knights, the best horse soldiers in Europe, many on their *destriers,* the horses specially bred to carry armored riders, armed with spears, swords and maces. Out from the three divisions, the barons and their military tenants, the knights who owe service for their lands, the volunteers and the mercenaries from many lands dash across the boggy valley and gallop up the slopes toward the English line ranged on the crest above. William, we may assume, spares nothing in his first assault. He sends all his horsemen to break the shield wall. The valley echoes with the noise and cries of war. Loud and far resound the bray of horns, the thunder of the horses' feet, the shouts of men bent on victory or death. The English housecarls stand behind their raised shields, awaiting the assault. Behind their ranks the massed rustics of the fyrd raise their spears. The floor of the valley is covered with horsemen, charging in squadrons and contingents, each knot of men following the pennon of their lord. They surge upward, breasting the slope ahead. "Out, out," shout the English as their enemies draw near. King Harold looks down over the heads of his men. Duke William watches from the slopes of Telham. It is the climax of his great adventure; England's diadem glitters before his eyes. The eager boldness of the Normans, according to William of Poitiers, carriers them up to the English line. The Bretons, riding up the easier slopes on the west, reach it first.

A rain of missiles greets the galloping horsemen. A hurricane of spears, hand axes, pointed sticks and heavy stones hurtle from the English line. The air is filled with a cloud of projectiles. Horses fall, their riders thrown to the ground and they roll together down the slope. Others, coming within range of the English, discharge their spears and javelins. The Englishmen above raise their shields, catching or turning away the flying missiles. Some find their mark, piercing the bodies of the tightly packed soldiers. The leading horsemen wheel about to allow those behind to join in the fray. *Olicrosse* and *Godemite,* shout the English. *Dex Aie,* cry the Normans in reply. The English resist valiantly, each man according to his strength. "You would have thought," says Wace, "to see our men overwhelmed by the death-dealing weight of missiles." Along the crest of the ridge the battle rages in all its fury. The English press forward, the invaders from over the sea ride up and away. The lines sway forward and back. Wace reports:

> Then came the cunning maneuvers, the rude shocks and strokes of the lance and blows of the sword, amongst the sergeants and soldiers, both English and Norman. When the English fall, the Normans shout. Each side taunts and defies the other, yet neither knoweth what the other said, and the Normans say the English bark, because they understand not their speech. Some wax strong, others weak; the brave exult but the cowards tremble, as men who are sore dismayed. The Normans press on the assault, and the English defend their position well; they pierce the hauberks, and cleave the shields; receive and return mighty blows. Again some press forward; others yield, and thus in various ways the struggle proceeds.

The English, however, in the words of William of Poitiers, have the advantage of the ground and are protected by remaining in their position in close order. They gain further superiority from their numbers, from the impregnable front they preserve and most of all from the manner in which their weapons find easy passage through the shields and armor of their enemies. Thus they bravely withstand and successively repulse those who are engaging them at close quarters, and inflict losses upon the men who are shooting missiles at them from a distance. Half a mile in length the battle rages along the crest of the ridge. The English line stands firm. The Continental horsemen surge up the slopes.

The toll of death is too great. The Bretons on the left flinch and turn away. They break in flight. Wheeling their horses, the knights flee down the slope. The panic spreads. Along the length of the ridge, the invaders stream back. The sight of their enemy, routed and in flight, is too much for the raw English shire levies. The men of the fyrd on the right of the line burst through the ranks of the housecarls and run down the slope in hot pursuit. That is one interpretation of the English sortie. In another, the order to break ranks and pursue is given by King Harold himself, who sees in the Breton flight the opportunity to deliver a counterstroke. Brave and impetuous as Harold was, it is unlikely that he would have attempted a counterattack so early in the battle; the retreat of the Bretons was more dramatic than catastrophic. To pursue them with foot soldiers was to court disaster.

The Bretons, riding down the slope, reach the valley bottom. The swampy ground slows their horses' hooves. The pursuers catch up. (According to William of Poitiers, the "greater part" of the English army sally out of their lines.) Amid the bogs and streams at the western end of the valley, the running footmen are a match for the impeded horsemen. The fyrd men stab and slash, and drag the riders from their mounts. From the maelstrom of death, the flying horsemen turn up the valley, seeking safety on the rising slopes of Telham Hill, where stands a crowd of varlets, the camp followers who have been left to guard the harness. The sight of the Breton debacle is too much for them. They turn to run. Bishop Eude rides to stop them. "Stand fast. Stand fast," he cries, "be quiet and move not. Fear nothing, for if God pleases we shall conquer yet." He gallops on to where the fight is fiercest.

From the mass of fugitives surging across the valley rises the cry that the Duke is dead. William is safe, but he knows how infectious is fear. Panic may spread along the line. His first assault on the English shield wall has collapsed. His army is in retreat; everywhere his knights are pouring back, the task too much for them. Thousands of English spearmen are rushing down the slopes, catching up with the fugitives. William's alert eye sees how the situation can be turned to advantage. Spurring his horse, he gallops to intercept the fleeing Bretons. William of Poitiers takes up the narrative:

> Seeing a large part of the hostile host pursuing his own troops, the prince thrust himself in front of those in flight, shouting at them and

> threatening them with his spear. Staying their retreat, he took his helmet, and standing before them bareheaded, he cried: "Look at me well. I am alive and by the grace of God I shall yet prove victor. What is this madness which makes you fly, and what way is open for your retreat? You are allowing yourselves to be pursued and killed by men whom you could slaughter like cattle. You are throwing away victory and lasting glory, rushing into ruin and incurring abiding disgrace. And all for naught, since by flight none of you can escape destruction."

With these words, says the Duke's chaplain, William restored his men's courage. Wielding his death-dealing sword, William set about to organize a counterattack. Meanwhile a terrible disaster had overcome some of the Normans in their retreat from the ridge. Wace tells the story:

> In the plain was a fosse, which the Normans had now behind them, having passed it in the fight without regarding it. But the English charged and drove the Normans before them, till they made them fall back upon this fosse, overthrowing into it horses and men. Many were to be seen falling therein, rolling one over the other, with their faces to the earth and unable to rise. Many of the English also, whom the Normans drew down along with them, died there.

The Tapestry depicts this disaster as occurring early in the battle. We see the pursuers and the pursued tumbling and floundering in a deep ravine, close by a mound, in which men and horses are hurled together in a confused mass, their agonized bodies contorted in the writhings and pangs of death. Lightly armed Englishmen are shown standing upon an elevated bank, hurling down darts on the Normans as they struggle and plunge in the fosse below. William of Poitiers describes a similar disaster but, in his account, it takes place at the end of the battle. Thus the two principal authorities are in conflict, and their contradictions raise the question of whether there were two fosse disasters, or one.

Like other visitors before me, I pondered the problem as I walked over the battlefield. If there were two separate disasters, each at a fosse, then there must have been two places where they could have occurred, the first early in the battle, following the Breton-Norman retreat, and the other late in the day, after dusk had fallen, during the Norman pursuit of the beaten English. The chroniclers could not have confused the two disasters because they happened at widely different times and, as the battle shifted, at widely separated places. According to the Tapestry, some Norman knights fell into a fosse or ravine during their retreat from the ridge. I looked, therefore, for such a spot in the center of the battlefield. On the slope from the ridge rose a mound or hillock, now covered by trees and shrubs. Beneath it, the ground was wet and boggy. Walking over it, I saw that it offered a trap to the unwary. In the center of the group of hillocks lay a deep and noisome dell, a place that fitted exactly the Tapestry's illustrations. It was easy to imagine the fleeing horsemen galloping over its deceptive slopes and falling into its "fosse-like" depths. How the second fosse has been located will be described later. My inspection of the battlefield confirmed that there were two such disasters, one only being known to the two principal authorities.

The Norman knights, it seems certain, plunged into the swampy dell at the hillock, which stands out about two hundred yards from the crest of the ridge. The disaster at this fosse was only part of the crisis which William faced. Most of the horsemen avoided this pitfall and they floundered on across the valley, where the duke halted their mad flight. He succeeded in rallying his knights and he led them to deliver a counterstroke on the pursuing English footmen, now exposed on open ground. Slashing and stabbing, the Normans rode through and around them, killing thousands, says William of Poitiers. None escaped. The Duke reaped advantage from the English sorties, for the shield wall was weakened by the loss of that number of men. He had surmounted the crisis of the battle, and the flight of the Bretons had given him an idea, one which he was to use later in the battle. Powerless to help unless they abandoned the ridge, the housecarls were forced to watch the slaughter of their men, the foolhardy rustics who had disobeyed orders.

In the valley below, the Normans and their allies regrouped their disorganized horsemen for fresh assault. While the knights reformed their ranks, the archers were sent forward to plague the English with their arrows. Wace reports, "The Norman archers with their bows shot thickly upon the English, but they covered themselves with their shields, so that the arrows could not reach their bodies, nor do any mischief, how true soever was their aim, or however well they shot." According to the *Draco Normannicus,* the archers ran out of arrows, for there were no English archers to return them. This faiure of the ammunition supply appears to have been only temporary, for we shall find Norman archers at work again later.

The archers withdraw and the knights, heartened by their success in the counterattack, furiously renew the assault on the ridge, on which stand the English hardly diminished in numbers, says William of Poitiers, who has previously recorded their severe losses. Perhaps the English ranks were reinforced by the stragglers, who, the chroniclers report, streamed in all day. Again, the Bretons, Normans and Frenchmen toil up the slopes towards the crest of the ridge. William of Poitiers tells the story:

> The English fought confidently with all their strength, striving in particular to prevent the attackers from penetrating within their ranks, which indeed were so closely massed together that even the dead had not space in which to fall. The swords of the bravest warriors hewed a gap in some places, and there they were followed by the men of Maine, by the French, by the Bretons and the men of Aquitaine, and by the Normans who showed the greatest valour. A certain Norman, Robert, son of Roger of Beaumont, found himself that day in battle for the first time; he was as yet but a young man, and he performed feats of valour worthy of perpetual remembrance. At the head of the troops which he commanded on the right wing, he attacked with the utmost vigour and success.

Wace is terser about this stage of the battle, saying only:

> The battle was up and down, this way and that, and no one knew who would conquer and win the land. Both sides stood so firm and fought so well, that no one could guess which would prevail.

From these brief reports we may conclude that confused mass attacks continued for some time. The English line was subjected to incessant assault by companies and squadrons of knights, grouped in twenties and fifties, who rode up to the English position, discharged their weapons and, when a gap was driven in the shield wall, plunged in, hacking and slashing with their swords and maces. Slowly the numbers on both sides diminished, as missiles found their marks and axes and swords slashed and cut. But the English line stood firm. It shortened, possibly, as the living pressed together to fill the places of the dead.

The chroniclers, particularly Wace, record several incidents of individual prowess and bravery on both sides, although we are left in the dark as to when they occurred. From Wace's story one interesting fact emerges. The lords and barons whom he names as fighting close to one another came from the same neighborhoods, which confirms that William grouped his men according to their places of origin. Occasionally, Wace gets his names wrong as, for example, when he refers to "old" Roger of Beaumont, when he means Roger's son Robert, who "threw himself into the fray, with his glittering sword." The English pierced his shield and killed his horse under him, and he would have been slain had not the Sire de Montfort (Hugh II) and the Sire William de Vezpont (who may in reality have been named Robert) come up with their strong force and bravely rescued him, though at the loss of many of their men, and mounted him on a fresh horse. Among the Normans who also fought well, Wace lists the men of Bessin; Neil of Saint-Sauveur, who exerted himself much to gain the goodwill of his duke and came with his sword to the rescue of many, and Raoul, Lord of Folgiers, who won great renown.

Wace's praises are not confined to the Normans; on the other side was an Englishman who much annoyed the French by continually assaulting them with a keen-edged hatchet. He had a helmet made of wood, which he had fastened to his coat and laced round his neck, so that no blows could reach his head. The ravage he was making was seen by a gallant Norman knight, who rode a horse that neither fire nor water would stop in its career when its lord urged it on. The knight spurred, and his horse carried him on till he charged the Englishman, striking him over the helmet, so that it fell down over his eyes; and as he stretched out his hand to raise it and uncover his face, the Norman cut off his right hand, so that the hatchet fell to the ground. Another Norman sprang forward and eagerly seized the prize with both hands, but he kept it for only a little time and paid dearly for it; for, as he stooped to pick up the hatchet, an Englishman struck him over the back with a long-handled axe, breaking all his bones, so that his entrails and lungs gushed forth. The knight of the good horse meanwhile returned without injury, but on his way he met another Englishman and rode him down, wounding him grievously and trampling him altogether underfoot.

Continuing with his anecdotes of the battle, Wace finds a story in the adventures of a vassal from the fief of Grandmesnil near Lisieux, who was in great peril when his horse ran away with him. He nearly fell off when it plunged over a bush and the reins broke. An Englishman, seeing his predicament, ran forward with his axe raised. The horse took fright and carried the Norman out of danger. Another Norman, Robert Fitz-Ernies, was not so fortunate. He made a gallant attempt to reach the English standard, forcing his way through the ranks with his sword. But the Englishmen surrounding it killed him with their bills. Those who sought him after the battle found him dead, lying at the standard's foot. Five knights, says Wace, the Sires of Combrai, Fontenei, Rebercial, Alnei and Molei, rode up to the English line, challenging King Harold to come out and fight, shouting: "Where is your king? He hath perjured himself to William. He is a dead man, if we find him."

Duke William, says Wace, fought gallantly, throwing himself in wherever the greatest press was, beating down many Englishmen, who found no rescue. Wherever the Duke went, Toesteny followed, bearing his gonfalon boldly aloft in the breeze. Whenever the Duke turned, he turned, and whenever the Duke stayed his course, he stopped also. The Duke's horse took him wherever he saw the most Englishmen, and he was followed by his own knights, who "to save their lord would have put their own bodies between him and the blows of the enemy." William, many chroniclers record, had three horses killed under him that day, yet he did not suffer the loss of a single drop of blood. The first time he was dismounted he called to a knight of Maine to give up his horse; the man refused and William struck him from the saddle and mounted his charger. When he was unhorsed again, he asked for the horse of Eustache of Boulogne, who gave it up gracefully, ordering one of his own men to make good his loss.

Duke William, says William of Poitiers, dominated the battle, checking his own men in flight, strengthening their spirit and sharing their dangers. He bade them come with him, more often than he ordered them to go in front of him. Thus it may be understood how he led them by his valor and gave them his courage. At the mere sight of this wonderful and redoubtable knight, many of his enemies lost heart even before they received a scratch. Thrice his horse fell under him; thrice he leaped upon the ground, and thrice he quickly avenged the death of his steed. It was here that one could see his prowess, and mark at once the strength of his arm and the height of his spirit. His sharp sword pierced shields, helmets and armor, and not a few felt the weight of his shield. His knights, seeing him thus on foot, were filled with wonder and, although many were wounded, they took new heart. Some, weakened by loss of blood, went on resisting, supported by their shields, and others, unable to carry on the struggle, urged on their comrades by voice and gesture to follow the Duke. "Surely," they cried, "you will not let victory slip from your hands." William came to the rescue of many.

William slew Gyrth, according to Wace and Ordericus Vitalis, who time his fall after the death of Harold, toward the end of the battle on the ridge. William forced his way toward the standard. His horse was killed by a spear thrust by Gyrth. William rose from the ground and felled Gyrth with his mace. In the Tapestry, Gyrth and his brother Leofwine fall early in the battle, at the hands of two unidentified knights. William of Poitiers passes over their death in silence, and we are left with no solution to the problem of when Harold's brothers, his two principal lieutenants, died, any more than we can be certain of the names of the King's other principal henchmen.

An Englishman, who is named "Ansgardus" by Guy of Amiens, is identified by Professor Freeman as the Staller Esegar, who is named "Ansgarus" in Domesday. He was Sheriff of Middlesex, and he may well have led his men in the battle. He was severely wounded and was carried to London, where he died on 1 November. The presence of two notable prelates, Leofric, Abbot of Peterborough, and the aged Aelfurg, Abbot of Winchester, Harold's uncle, who brought with him twelve monks, their cowls concealed beneath their helmets, is well attested. Aelfurg died in the battle, and Leofric returned home severely wounded. Several other Englishmen are named in Domesday as having fought at Hastings, among them Sheriff Godric, Lord of Fifhide, and Thurkill of Kingston, both from Berkshire, and Eadric, a deacon from East Anglia, who was also killed.

The identities of the Normans and their allies who fought at Hastings is a far more controversial matter. The explosive problem of the names of the Conqueror's companions is discussed in the Appendix.

It is remarkable that no notable Norman, Frenchman or Breton appears to have been killed or even severely wounded in the battle, although the Tapestry depicts a number of Normans, or their allies, being slain. Yet the invaders must have suffered severe casualties, for they were the aggressors and the majority of the English soldiers appear to have perished, along with their chiefs. William seems to have marched on to London with the strength of his army little diminished. No previous commentator has remarked on this strange anomaly, one which tends to confirm the view that the Normans confined their assaults against the shield wall chiefly to long-range tactics and missile fire, and that the principal English casualties occurred in the various sorties and from the high-angle arrow fire which decided the battle.

The battle on the ridge raged for hours. The English army was still formidable and very difficult to overwhelm, records William of Poitiers. It was a battle of a new type, he says, with one side vigorously attacking and the other resisting, as if rooted to the ground. "They were ever ready with their steel, these sons of the old Anglo-Saxon race, the most dauntless of men," he remarks. Ordericus Vitalis speaks of the valor of the English and how "their glory raged." The English stood firm, observes Wace. Of King Harold, he states that none came within his reach with impunity, for he brought down both horse and rider at one blow. The English double-bladed axe impressed the chroniclers. Woe befell the Normans who ventured near its sweeping blow, observes Wace. At a single blow an Englishman cleft his enemy from head to breast. The Tapestry depicts how the English wielded their axes. With one exception, the housecarls held its five-foot shaft with the left hand above the right, and struck from the left shoulder so as to take their adversary on the right side, where he was least protected by his shield. When wielding their weapon, the axe-men either laid aside their shields or slung them over their shoulders. Against the stoutly held shieldwall, the Norman horsemen proved singularly ineffective. "Never," says Sir Charles Oman, "had continental horsemen met such infantry before."

Thirteen

The Archers

The day was now far advanced and the shield wall still held steadfast. The Norman javelin attacks and the heavy loss incurred in pursuit of the Bretons had only weakened it. As long as the English stood firm on the crest of the ridge, keeping their position, they were invincible. Could they be induced to leave it, to charge down again into the valley where their foot-soldiers were easy prey for the Norman horsemen? About 3 P.M., says Wace (and he is supported by the best authorities), the Normans staged a feigned flight to draw the English from the ridge. Few modern historians agree that this daring stratagem was planned and carried out. The chroniclers invented it, they say, in order to disguise the unpalatable fact that, at some stage of the battle, the brave Normans were routed by the English as the Bretons had been earlier in the day. The reasons they give for rejecting the story of the pretended Norman flight appear to be overwhelming, but their arguments may well be fallacious.

Such a complicated stratagem in the heat of battle, they claim, would have been too risky, for panic is infectious, and the feigned flight could have degenerated into a complete rout. It is a military maxim that troops, once committed to an attack, cannot easily be made to change direction. How could the order to wheel about and flee have been conveyed to hundreds, perhaps thousands, of men engaged in personal hand-to-hand combat? And how could it have been signalled without the English guessing what was afoot? The English, it is argued, had been caught once, and they would have been wary of again being enticed down the slopes. After the disaster following the Breton flight, King Harold would have taken steps to ensure that his order to stand firm was not again disobeyed. To the argument that the Normans staged a successful feigned flight at Arques in 1053 and that the Normans in Sicily had adopted the same stratagem, the objectors counter that the circumstances at Arques and Hastings were different. At Arques, the Norman knights sallied out, fully briefed, to draw the French into a carefully prepared ambush several miles away.

Valid as these objections appear, they fail to take into consideration the daring and the cunning of the Normans and the desperate situation they faced at Hastings. To have staged a feigned flight need not have been so difficult as it sounds. There must have been many pauses in the battle when the Normans and their allies were grouped together on the floor of the valley three hundred yards from the English position, and, we recall, the hero of Arques, Walter Giffard, was at William's side at Hastings. The ruse could have been organized as a concerted maneuver, and it did not require many men. It needed to be put into operation only on a small section of the front, while the rest of the Normans, Frenchmen and Bretons distracted the English by pressing home their attacks, as Guy of Amiens implies did happen. The chroniclers are as one in saying that the stratagem, the classic incident of the battle, was executed, and they indicate that it took place on the right, or right center of the line, for, according to *The Chronicle of Battle Abbey,* Eustace of Boulogne was involved, and the cutting-off of the pursuers was done, in the words of Guy of Amiens and Wace, by the French and the mercenaries, who were stationed on the right wing.

The Normans beguiled the English from their vantage point, wheeling about, retreating in seeming disorder down the slope and across the valley in the direction of the Hastings road, where the valley narrows, in order to entice their pursuers toward the French knights who were lying in wait on the lower slopes of Telham, the height of which gave their descent added momentum. At the critical moment, they charged down, inflicting immense slaughter on the disorderly mass below.

The Chronicle of Battle Abbey states:

> By a preconceived scheme the duke feigned a retreat with his army, and Eustace, the valiant Count of Boulogne, nimbly following the rear of the English, who were scattered in pursuit, rushed upon them with his powerful troops.

In his account, William of Poitiers says:

> Realizing that they could not without severe loss overcome an enemy massed so strongly in close formation, the Normans and their allies feigned flight and simulated a retreat, for they recalled that only a short while ago their flight had given them an advantage. The barbarians, thinking victory within their grasp, shouted with triumph, and heaping insults on our men, threatened utterly to destroy them. Several thousand of them, as before, gave rapid pursuit to those whom they thought to be in flight; but the Normans suddenly wheeling their horses surrounded them and cut down their pursuers so that not one was left alive. Twice was this ruse employed with the utmost success, and then they attacked those that remained with the utmost fury.

Wace, as usual, is more loquacious, telling the story in considerable detail:

> The Normans saw that the English defended themselves well, and were so strong in their position that they could do little against them, so they consulted together privily, and arranged to draw off, and to pretend to flee, till the English should pursue and scatter themselves over the field; for they saw that if they could once get their enemies to break their ranks, they might be attacked and discomfited much more easily. And as they said, so they did. The Normans by little and little fled, the English following them. As the one fell back, the other pressed after; and when the Frenchmen retreated, the English thought and cried out, that the men of France fled, and would never return.
>
> Thus they were deceived by the pretended flight, and great mischief thereby befell them; for if they had not moved from their position, it is not likely that they would have been conquered at all; but like fools they broke their line and pursued.
>
> The Normans were to be seen following up their stratagem, retreating slowly so as to draw the English further on. As still they flee, the English pursue; they push out their lances and stretch forth

their hatchets, following the Normans, as they go, rejoicing in the success of their scheme, and scattering themselves over the plain. And the English meantime jeered and insulted their foes with words. "Cowards," they cried, "You come hither in an evil hour, wanting our lands, and seeking to seize our property, fools that you were to come. Normandy is too far off, and you will not easily reach it. It is of little use to run back; unless you can cross the sea at one leap, or can drink it dry, your sons and daughters are lost to you."

The Normans bore it all, but in fact they knew not what the English said; their language seemed like the baying of dogs, which they could not understand. At length they stopped and turned round, determined to recover their ranks, and the barons might be heard calling *Dex Aie,* for a halt.

Then the Normans resumed their former position, turning their faces towards the enemy; and the men were to be seen facing round and rushing onwards to a fresh melée, the one party attacking the other, this man striking, another pressing onwards, One hits, another misses; one flies, another pursues; one is aiming a stroke, while another discharges his blow. Norman strives with Englishman again, and aims his blows afresh. One flies, another pursues swiftly; the combatants are many, the play wide, the battle and the melée fierce. On every hand they fight hard, the blows are heavy, and the struggle becomes fierce.

Wace tells the story of several individual encounters:

The Normans were playing their part well when an English knight came rushing up, having in his company a hundred men, furnished with various arms. He wielded a northern hatchet, with the blade a full foot long, and was well-armed after his manner, being tall and bold, and of noble carriage. In the front of the battle, where the Normans thronged most, he came bounding on, swifter than the stag, many Normans falling before him and his company. He rushed straight upon a Norman who was armed and riding on a war-horse, and tried with his hatchet of steel to cleave his helmet; but the blow miscarried, and the sharp blade glanced down before the saddle bow, driving through the horse's neck, down to the ground, so that both horse and master fell together to the earth. I know not whether the Englishman struck another blow, but the Normans who saw the stroke were astonished, and were about to

> abandon the assault, when Roger de Montgomery came galloping up, with his lance set, and heeding not the long two-handed axe, which the Englishman wielded aloft, struck him down, and left him stretched upon the ground. Then Roger cried "Frenchmen, strike, the day is ours." And again a fierce melée was to be seen, with many a blow of lance and sword; the English still defending themselves, killing the horses and cleaving the shields. . . .
>
> There was a French soldier of noble mien, who sat his horse gallantly. He spied two Englishmen who were also carrrying themselves boldly. They were both men of great worth, and had become companions in arms and fought together, the one protecting the other. They bore two long and broad bills, and did great mischief to the Normans, killing both men and horses. The French soldier looked at them and their bills, and was sore alarmed, for he was afraid of losing his good horse, the best he had, and would have willingly have turned to some other quarter, if it would not have looked like cowardice. He soon, however, recovered his courage, and spurring his horse, gave him the bridle, and galloped swiftly forward. Fearing the two bills, he raised his shield by the straps and struck one of the Englishmen with his lance on the breast, so that the iron passed out at his back. At the moment he fell, the lance broke, and the Frenchman seized the mace that hung at his right side, and struck the other Englishman a blow that completely fractured his skull.

Readers can judge for themselves whether the Normans fled in uncontrolled panic or withdrew "according to plan." Either way, the result was the same. The English line had been further weakened. Again, Harold and his stalwarts had been forced to watch, impotent to help, as the disobedient rustics rushed to their doom. But the shield wall stood firm; the standard fluttered in the breeze; the heroic band of housecarls held its ground, still formidable and full of fight. The Normans had failed to break the dauntless phalanx; nothing in the evidence suggests that the housecarls joined in the pursuit of the fleeing Bretons or Normans. The shadows were beginning to lengthen, and the day of St. Calixtus was nearly done; the sun inclined toward the west. If, as Wace says, the feigned flight was conceived about 3 P.M., there were barely ninety minutes of daylight left, for the sun, astronomical tables show, sank that night at 5:04 P.M.

In my interpretation of the battle, the Normans were beaten. All day long they had ridden up to the ridge, discharged their weapons and withdrawn. There had been many personal combats; gaps had been torn in the English line, and bands of Normans had penetrated, only to be thrown out again. The housecarls had been forced to close up and shorten their ranks and to concentrate round the standard on the crown of the ridge, and there were now fewer men massed behind them. Casualties on both sides were heavy; the slopes from the ridge were strewn with corpses; riderless horses careened madly across the valley. Down from the impenetrable ridge ran a bloody trail of death; the air was filled with the groans of the wounded and the screams of the dying. The Norman knights were exhausted, their horses blown. Everyone was utterly fatigued. They had been fighting since 9 A.M., but had been in the saddle since long before dawn.

William despaired. His brave and experienced knights, riding their trained war-horses, had failed to break the English line. The instrument with which he had expected to conquer England had cracked. He had miscalculated; his noble knights were more than a match for the chivalry of Europe, but they had failed to dislodge disciplined, well-armed infantry drawn up on a strong position. The invaders faced defeat. They were not in immediate danger, for the English were in no condition to counterattack. But King Harold could withdraw under the cover of night and, having learned his lesson, he could bide his time, which would end the invasion. While he raised a fresh army, the Normans would be bottled up in Hastings, blockaded by the English fleet, unable to retreat across the sea or to receive reinforcements, their army wasting and starving. If they sallied out again to bring Harold to battle, he might lead them to destruction in the trackless forests of the Weald. It would be the Battle of Teutobergerwald all over again. As the Saxons' famous ancestor Arminius had destroyed the straggling legions of Varus in A.D. 9, so could Harold have destroyed Duke William's troops in 1066. William's plan to bring Harold to quick, decisive battle was crumbling into ruins. The great adventure, the conquest of England, was a shattered wreck.

William rode among his men. The horses hung their heads; the knights sprawled dejectedly in their saddles. Only the archers stood fresh and alert, their ranks intact. They had had a disappointing day, for their arrows, fired upward, had driven into the English shields massed above them. Few of their shafts had been returned, and their ammunition was running low. William, all historians agree, was a man of flexible, elastic mind, capable of thinking out the logical consequences of acts, and an experienced and versatile soldier. It is not unreasonable, therefore, to attribute to William himself the great idea that turned defeat into victory. His archers' arrows had been aimed directly at the Englishmen's bodies; shot at that angle they had done little harm. Supposing the archers fired upward, in a high sweeping trajectory? The missiles would descend vertically on the unprotected faces of the English. A cloud of high-angle flying arrows would blind them to the danger from the front, as the horsemen charged beneath the barrage of missiles.

William called the captain of the archers, of the men of Evreux and Louviers who had learned their craft in the woods and forests of Normandy. Had their bows sufficient range to shoot over the Englishmen's shields, high in the sky? Were there enough arrows in reserve for a final assault? The velocity of the arrows, fired in that way, would be less, but they would reach their target, replied the captain. Yes, they had sufficient arrows for what the Duke wanted done. William turned to his barons and to the leaders of the volunteers and the mercenaries. Were their knights capable of one last, supreme effort, a final dash up to slopes to the ridge? Yes, replied the men who had come to England to win wealth and renown.

William set the field. He arranged the archers in a long, loose line, leaving gaps through which the horsemen could ride. He marshalled his knights on the floor of the valley. At his command, the parallel lines moved up the slopes ahead, the archers running swiftly, the horses breaking into a trot. At one hundred yards short of the English line, the archers halted. Crouching beneath their quivers, they loosed their arrows, elevating their bows. As the cloud of arrows hissed upwards, the knights spurred their horses to a gallop, charging between the archers and up the slope toward the ridge, under the cover of the arrows. The arrows swept over the massed line of shields, and in their falling, records Wace, they struck the heads and faces of the English and put out the eyes of many. "All feared to open their eyes or leave their faces unguarded." The arrows flew thicker than rain before the wind: "Fast," he says, "sped the shafts which the English called, from the sound they made, 'Wibetes.'" To protect their faces from the falling shower, the Englishmen were forced to raise their shields. This prevented them from wielding their axes, and it exposed their bodies to the thrusts of lances. The horsemen charged in under the creeping barrage.

One random arrow, pregnant with fate, shot upward into the air and struck King Harold above his right eye, putting it out. In his agony, says Wace, he drew the arrow and threw it way, breaking it with his hands, and the pain to his head was so great that he leaned upon his shield. So the English were wont to say, and still say to the French, that the arrow was well shot that was sent against the King and that the archer who thus put out Harold's eye won them great glory.

The Tapestry depicts King Harold, his shield bristling with arrows, the fatal arrow piercing his eye. Convulsively he clutches its shaft, breaking it in his agonized grasp. His axe falls from his nerveless hand. In mortal agony, he sinks to the ground at the foot of the standard. He still breathes.

Reaching the crest of the ridge, the horsemen pushed home their advantage against the English ranks, now shortened and concentrated round the crown, which enabled the knights from the west to gain the ridge and ride against the English right flank, no longer anchored on the steep bank to the northwest. Encircling the gallant band round the standard, the invaders charged in, pushing their way through gaps, penetrating and thrusting on. They threw, struck and pierced, says William of Poitiers. The Duke, leading a great troop of knights, all plying their blows and returning blow for blow, strove to reach the standard. Wace tells the story of William's encounter with an Englishman:

> One of them was a man of great strength, a wrestler, who did great mischief to the Normans with his hatchet; all feared him for he struck down a great many Normans. The duke spurred on his horse, and aimed a blow at him, but he stooped, and so escaped the stroke, then jumping to one side, he lifted his hatchet aloft, and as the duke bent to avoid the blow, the Englishman boldly struck him on the head, and beat in his helmet, though without doing much injury. He was very near falling, however, but bearing on his stirrups he recovered himself immediately; and when he thought to revenge himself on the vagabond by killing him, the rogue had escaped,

> dreading the duke's blow. He ran back amongst the English, but he was not safe even there, for the Normans seeing him, pursued and caught him, and having pierced him through and through with their lances, left him dead on the ground.

In one place where the battle was thickest, the men of Kent and Essex, says Wace, fought wondrously well and made the Normans retreat. "And when the duke saw his men fall back, and the English triumphing over them, his spirit rose high, and he seized his shield by the straps, and took his lance, which a vassal handed him." Leading his men, William rushed on the ranks of the English, and his knights, breaking by the weight of their good horses and by their blows the press of the enemy, scattered the crowd before them. Many Englishmen fell and were trampled by the horses; others fled or crawled around upon the earth, unable to rise. One Englishman watched the Duke and plotted to kill him. He would have struck him with his lance, but he could not, for the Duke struck him first and felled him to the earth. Many of the richest and noblest Englishmen fell in that place, states Wace, but still others rallied, smiting down those they could reach, and continuing the combat as best they could, beating down the riders and killing the horses. Loud was the clamor and great the slaughter; the living marched over the dead, and each side became weary of striking. Wace carries on his report:

> He charged on who could, and he who could no longer strike, still pressed forward. The strong struggled with the strong; some failed, others triumphed. The cowards fell back, the brave pressed on; and sad was his fate who fell in the midst, for he had little chance of rising again, and many in truth fell who never rose at all, being crushed under the throng.

The Normans and their French allies press up to the crown of the ridge, which is still defended by a ring of housecarls. Hacking and slashing, they thrust toward the English standard. By its foot lies King Harold, suffering grievously from his wound. Four knights rush upon his prostrate body. One stabs the dying king in the breast, another strikes off his head, a third tears the entrails from his body, a fourth severs his leg. The perpetrator of this last outrage, states William of Malmesbury, was expelled in ignominy from the Norman army. He cannot be identified, but the other men were, Guy of Amiens says, knights from Ponthieu, near Amiens; Bolbec, near Havre, and Montfort by Pont Audemer, by whom he may have meant a son of Guy of Ponthieu, Harold's erstwhile captor, Walter Giffard and Hugh de Montfort. Eustace, Count of Boulogne, appears to have been among the troop, which indicates, along with the other names, that the men who killed King Harold and mutilated his corpse, were Frenchmen. The Tapestry depicts the scene of outrage; an unnamed knight is shown hacking his left leg.

King Harold is dead, the battle lost. For a time the English thegns and the remnant of the gallant housecarls fight on around the standard. Quarter is neither asked nor given. No prisoners are taken by the Normans. At last the English weary; the survivors of the nobility of England fall beneath the standard. The Normans tear it down and wave it exultantly. The rustics of the fyrd retreat toward the back of the ridge along the spur leading to the rear.

William of Poitiers takes up the narrative:

> Evening was now falling, and the English saw that they could not hold out much longer against the Normans. They knew they had lost a greater part of their army, and they knew also that their king, with two of his brothers and many of their greatest men, had fallen. Those who remained were almost exhausted, and they realised they could expect no more help. They saw the Normans, whose numbers had not been much diminished, attack them with even greater fury than at the beginning of the battle, as if the day's fighting had actually increased their vigour.
>
> Dismayed at the implacable bearing of the duke, who spared none who came up against him and whose prowess could not rest until victory was won, they began to fly as swiftly as they could, some on horseback, some on foot, some along the roads, but most over the trackless country. Many lay on the ground bathed in blood, others who struggled to their feet found themselves too weak to escape, while a few although disabled were given strength to move by fear. Many left their corpses in the depths of the forest, and others were found by their pursuers lying by the roadside. Although ignorant of the countryside, the Normans eagerly carried on the pursuit, and striking the rebels in the back, brought a happy end to this famous

victory. Many fallen to the ground were trampled to death by the hooves of runaway horses.

The Tapestry shows the English flying, some on the horses of their leaders and those that had brought the housecarls to the battle, hotly pursued by the Normans, among them a number of archers, who have also horsed themselves. Other Normans strip the dead of their valuable mail shirts.

Most of the English, says Wace, did not stop until they reached London, crying out that the Normans were following. The press to cross the deep River Thames was so great that the bridge broke under the throng, and many fell into the water; not an unlikely accident, for London Bridge was probably a fragile structure until it was rebuilt by Henry I. But not all the English fled from the scene of the battle. A number turned at bay to fight a spirited rearguard action. In the hour of their triumph, the Normans and their French allies suffered a severe reverse, losing more men than at any time during the battle at a spot that became known in the course of time as "Malfosse," a place of evil repute.

It has been remarked previously that the chroniclers of the battle describe two "fosse" disasters, one of which took place early in the day on the southern slopes of the ridge, following the Breton retreat, and the other late in the day, after dusk had fallen, along the line of the English retreat. The place of the first disaster suffered by the Normans has been identified as the Hillock, the mound surrounding a deep dell, which is exactly where we would expect to find it. The identification of the scene of the second disaster is more difficult, for we know only that it occurred somewhere north of the ridge and that Eustace of Boulogne and his French knights were concerned in it. The difference between time and direction proves that there were two similar disasters, but we need to be wary of the stories told, for we cannot always be certain to which disaster a particular chronicler refers. Each heard about one disaster, without knowing where or when it occurred.

Careful study of the chroniclers indicates that the second disaster befell Frenchmen during the pursuit of the fleeing enemy, when the impetuous knights fell and floundered in a deep declivity, on the farther bank of which English soldiers had rallied. Where was Malfosse? Four detectives have selected four different places. Like them, we need to start with the narratives of the five chroniclers who seem to be writing about the disaster late in the day.

William of Poitiers, having described how the English took flight in all directions and how the Normans, though unacquainted with the country, pursued anxiously, says:

> Some of those who retreated took courage to renew the struggle on more favourable ground. This was a steep valley intersected with numerous ditches.

William of Jumièges states:

> The long grass hid from the Normans an ancient causeway into which they were suddenly precipitated, and into it they fell with their horses and armour, one on top of the other, suddenly without warning.

William of Malmesbury relates of the English:

> . . . getting possession of an eminence, they drove down the Normans, when roused with indignation and anxiously striving to gain the higher ground, into the valley beneath, where, hurling their javelins and rolling down stones on them as they lay below, they destroyed them to a man. Besides, by a short passage, with which they were acquainted, avoiding a deep ditch, they trod underfoot such a multitude of their enemies in that place, that they made the hollow level with the plain, by the heaps of carcasses.

The Norman monk, Ordericus Vitalis, who may have seen the spot on a visit to the Abbey, tells us:

> But the growing grass covered an ancient causeway (*antiquum agger*) where the charging Normans fell headlong in large numbers, with their horses and arms; and this, as one after another unexpectedly fell, destroyed them in turn. This certainly renewed the confidence of the fleeing English. Realising the opportunity given them by a steep bank and by frequent ditches, they unexpectedly halted, pulled themselves together, and inflicted great slaughter on the Normans.

The Chronicle of Battle Abbey, which was written before 1180, has the advantage of its authors' acquaintance with the district and almost certain knowledge of the place before its location was forgotten. It states:

> . . . after countless of the wretched English had been struck down in the battle, or rather in the flight, a supreme calamity was exposed for all to see. Between the two armies lay a dreadful chasm, of broad extent, when seen at close quarters, a wide open ravine formed either by a natural cleft in the ground or perhaps by being hollowed out by storms, yet so overgrown in its vast expanse by bushes and brambles that it was not discernible, so that it destroyed large numbers, especially of the pursuing Normans. For, as in their wild unwitting charge they galloped headlong into this place, they perished terribly, dashed to pieces. And so this abyss is to this day called by the name derived from this disaster—Malfosse.

Several clues emerge from these accounts: the pursuers fall from, clearly not into, a raised causeway, the word *agger* denoting something artificial, and *antiquum* implying that it was old and decayed. This raised causeway ran alongside, or crossed, a deep ravine, the dangers of which could be avoided by a "short passage" which was known to the local men. This dreadful chasm was concealed by bushes, and its farther bank was steep. There the English turned on their pursuers, riding hard in the gathering gloom. The English flight, we may conclude, was in a northerly direction from the ridge, up the spur toward Caldbec Hill. From there the fugitives could have taken either of the roads leading to the northwest and northeast, or they could have spread out across country by little-known tracks and byways. Few, if any, would have been able to escape to the west or the east, as the Bretons were advancing from one side and the French from the other.

The search for the place named Malfosse is based on five source documents: *Domesday Book,* which describes the 735 acres owned by the Abbey in 1086; *The Chronicle of Battle Abbey,* which tells the history of the Abbey and its lands, but which does not state where Malfosse was; the deeds of the Abbey, which have been since 1928 in the Huntington Library, San Marino, California; *Thorpe's Catalogue of the Deeds,* made in 1835; Dugdale's *Monasticon* (III, 255), which lists by name the fields granted in 1538 to Sir Anthony Browne; the Abbey estate maps of 1724 and 1811; the *Manor Rental of* 1838; *Gleanings Respecting Battel and its Abbey,* published by F. W. Ticehurst, Battle, 1841, and the Battle Abbey Tithe Award Map of 1858. These documents provide the only information upon which search for the site can be based. The first two show that, although the ridge and the spur were uncultivated scrub land, the low ground around the place of battle, including the fringes of the Weald north of Caldbec Hill, was both inhabited and cultivated in 1066.

Three of the sites that have been identified as the Malfosse fail to fulfill the required conditions. Professor Freeman chose the precipitous bank on the left rear of the ridge, a steep descent down which the pursuing Frenchmen might have galloped to their doom but which lacks a steep bank on which the fleeing English could have rallied and which has no ancient causeway.

Mr. M. A. Lower in 1851, though he could find no place near Battle which could be called a "dreadful precipice," nevertheless selected for Malfosse the banks of a boggy rivulet, which runs to the northwest of the town about 1,200 yards behind the ridge. He based his choice of the spot, which he thought might have been an overgrown swamp in the eleventh century, on an ancient deed that records the grant to the Abbey in 1279 of nine acres of land called Wincestrecroft "in Mainfosse." He located Wincestrecroft in the wrong place.

The Hon. Francis Baring, employing Thorpe's summaries of seven deeds, located the ravine of evil repute in the steep banks of another stream, which runs due west of the ridge and about 800 yards from its crown. For centuries it had been called "Mansers Shaw," into which he thought the old name had been corrupted, incorrectly, for it derived its name from a person called Fitz-Manser. The errors of Baring's solution have been exposed by Mr. C. T. Chevallier, until 1958, Clerk of the Battle District Council, who lectured on the location of Malfosse in 1953 to the Battle and District Historical Society and with whom I conferred in 1964.

The ancient deeds, observes Mr. Chevallier (who obtained photocopies from California), show that parcels of land "in Maufosse" were granted to the Abbey in exchange for other land by private owners in the thirteenth century. Mr. Baring's location was ruled out for two reasons. The Abbey kept all the fields around Mansers Shaw strictly in its own hands, and no one was permitted to let or grant them. Although "Mansers Shaw" might be a corruption of "Manfosse" (as Thorpe mistakenly read it), it could not have been derived from "Maufosse," as the monks had written it.

The reference to "Maufosse" in the thirteenth-century deeds, at a time when the location of Malfosse was probably still known, convinced Mr. Chevallier that the ravine lay somewhere within the original estate, which ran for one and a half miles around the Abbey and to the north, on the line of English flight. There can be little doubt that Mr. Chevallier has located Malfosse. He succeeded, where his predecessors had failed, by looking in the right place and by re-examining the ancient deeds, which contain the following:

> In 1240 Reginald de Camera and his wife granted to the abbey "six acres of land and a wood in Maufosse," together with a right of way "alongside the great trench" (magnum fossatum). In 1245 Adam Picot and his wife granted "nine acres of our land and our wood in Maufosse." In 1279 Adam Picot the younger confirmed the grant, and the deed mentions rent being payable "for a certain piece of land which remains to me from my mother's inheritance lying to the east of the said nine acres in the long croft called Wincestrecroft."

Mr. Chevallier found Wincestrecroft referred to again in a deed dated 1332, in which the rector of Whatlington (a village to the northeast of Battle) granted to Stephen Pessoner, the beadle of Battle, three crofts, one of which was called Northrode and another Wincestrecroft. The name "Northrode" implies proximity to the road that ran from Battle to Whatlington. This clue led Mr. Chevallier to seek Malfosse north of Caldbec Hill, where, according to local legend, William "called back" his men from pursuit of the English. The deed referred to "a croft leading to a pool"; in a field, named "Hickets Croft" on the manor map of 1724, he found a spring. If this field was the original Wincestrecroft, the fields adjacent were those described "in Maufosse." This assumption could be tested; one field was named Pycott's on the 1724 map, which was closely akin to "Picots." This, and other fields lying to the north of Virgin's Lane, appeared to constitute "six" and "nine" acres, and they abutted, Mr. Chevallier knew, on a "great trench," which fulfilled the conditions of Malfosse.

Oakwood Gill runs through a deep gulley, fed by the waters of several ditches which unite to form a "ravine," the bottom of which is obscured by brambles, trees and shrubs. Its far bank is high and steep. The London Turnpike Road (A 21), built in 1836, crossed the ravine. It would be a surprising coincidence, thought Mr. Chevallier, if the road had been constructed directly on top of an ancient causeway that had also crossed the stream at that point. Yet that is precisely what had happened. On the 1724 map, two fields south of the gill, named Fotherland and Pycotts, are separated, not by a continuous line denoting a hedge, but by a dotted line indicating a path, which appeared to be an extension of the track running northward from Virgin's Lane. Mr. Chevallier found a further clue in the word "Fotherland," for the old English word "Fotherford" meant a ford or bridge that could carry a cartload. But if the gill had been crossed by an ancient causeway at that point, where had a causeway led? In the Abbey chronicle and other documents, Mr. Chevallier found reference to a farm bearing the old English name of "Dunintune," which lay just north of Oakwood Gill, to which the causeway probably gave access. Having established the onetime existence of a causeway over the gill, he sought to discover why it might have fallen into disuse and become *antiqua* by 1066. The old farm to which it led, he found, had been extended before the Conquest to the northeast, up to an existing road which would have provided a new entrance, thus causing the ancient causeway to fall into disuse. In this ruinous state and covered with thick grass, it would have been, in the darkness, a death trap for horsemen; riding hard, they fell off it, one upon another, into the ravine.

Mr. Chevallier's discovery makes possible the reconstruction of the disaster. The French knights, led by Eustace of Boulogne, pursued the fleeing English down the northern slopes of Caldbec Hill. They were followed by Duke William. Some Englishmen, probably local men, rallied on the far bank of Oakwood Gill, which runs about 600 yards north of Caldbec Hill, the deep ravine of which they avoided by a "short passage" known to them. William of Poitiers states that the Duke did not turn from his course when he saw the enemy's troops rallying. He thought, probably, that reinforcements had joined his foes.

The French knights did not see the danger ahead, for the ravine was overgrown with brambles, and the ancient causeway on which they were riding was deep in long grass. In the fading light, they crashed headlong into the deep ravine, where they were dashed to pieces and killed by the Englishmen, who threw down javelins and stones. Eustace himself, with fifty knights, turned in flight, meeting the Duke who, according to William of Poitiers, "called to him with a harsh voice," as he was about to give the signal for retreat. Eustace rode up to the Duke and "said in his ear" that he ought to retire "since he would court death if he went forward." At the moment he uttered these words, Eustace was struck between the shoulders "with such force that blood gushed out of his mouth and nose, and, half-dead, he only made his escape with the aid of his followers." The Duke, however, states William of Poitiers, was above all fear and dishonor, and he attacked and beat back his enemies, who were very close presumably, for otherwise Eustace could not have been struck so hard. "In this dangerous place," states the Duke's chaplain, "many Norman nobles were killed, since the nature of the ground did not permit them to display their prowess to full advantage."

Having mopped up this last pocket of English resistance, the Normans withdrew to Caldbec Hill, the name of which was once believed to signify "Call-back Hill," denoting the spot from which William called back his soldiers from pursuit of the English, whereas the true etymological meaning is *cald-bec,* referring to the cold spring that gushes still from a cavernous recess on the eastern slopes of the hill. Here the Normans, it is believed, raised a cairn of stones to serve as a monument to their victory and lit a beacon, the reason why the hill was subsequently named *Mont-joie*. There is a tradition also that a large tree, which is believed to have grown on the site of the present Rural District Council offices at the intersection of the roads that lead into Battle High Street, was once named "Watch Oak," because there Harold first pitched his standard.

Having regained his superiority, records William of Poitiers, William returned to the battlefield, where "he could not gaze without pity on the carnage, although the slain were evil men." The bloodstained battleground, he says, was covered with the flower of the youth and nobility of England. In his pride, says Wace, the Duke ordered his gonfalon to be brought and set up on high where the English standard had stood. He commanded his tent to be erected among the dead, and there he ordered his supper. "What are you about?" objected William Giffard. "Many an Englishman," he protested, "lies bloody and mingled with the dead, but yet sound, or not wounded, and besmirched with gore, tarrying of his own accord and meaning to rise at night and escape in the darkness." The English would delight in taking revenge, he warned. To his urgings that the Duke should move his tent elsewhere, where he could be guarded by two thousand armed men, William turned a deaf ear. He called his esquires, who took off his armor; he thanked the knights around him and, having eaten and drunk, he flung himself down to sleep.

William of Poitiers concludes his story of the Battle of Hastings with the remark, "Thus fortune crowned the triumph of William." Whether or not the Duke's chaplain spoke metaphorically, he indeed told the truth. Seldom can a victory have been more fortuitous. Because the wind had delayed William, he had landed in England after Hardrada, whom Harold was forced to fight first. Exhausted after the five hundred-mile march, their ranks thinned by their great victory in the North, the English housecarls had been forced by Harold's impetuosity to fight a second major battle within two weeks. Even so, it had been a "damned close run thing," as the Duke of Wellington remarked after his victory at Waterloo. The Englishmen had fought the Normans to a standstill. Only his clever ruse of high-angle fire had saved William from defeat. If the wind had shifted to the south a few weeks earlier, the Normans might have encountered the whole army of southern England, rather than a scratch force hurriedly assembled to support the thinned ranks of the housecarls. William's great victory was due to mere chance, the vagaries of the English weather. The decisive battle had been won; the perjured usurper had been slain. William had yet to win the crown that he believed was his by right.

Fourteen

The King

The exhausted Normans bestirred themselves at break of day. The grey light of dawn on that Sunday morning disclosed the full extent of their victory. The hill of slaughter was heaped with corpses. Its crown, where the dragon of Wessex had fluttered, was piled with dead. "The bloodstained battlefield," states William of Poitiers, who may have visited it, "was covered with the corpses of the youth and nobility of England." The streams around the hill ran red with blood, according to *The Chronicle of Battle Abbey;* its compiler may have drawn upon the reminiscences of William Faber. No chronicler mentions the succor of any wounded men. The Normans, says the Duke's chaplain, having despoiled the bodies of their enemies, buried those of their own comrades. William ordered the monk, who prior to the departure from Dives had written down the names of the chief men of the army, to call the roll and ascertain who had fallen and who had survived. This roll may have been the famous Roll of the Conqueror's Companions, which was kept at the Abbey until it disappeared in the fourteenth century. The Duke walked over the field, searching for the bodies of his friends, whom he ordered buried in the bowels of the earth. Bishop Eude sang a mass for the souls of the departed.

The Duke allowed the women of the surrounding countryside to remove the bodies of their husbands, sons, brothers and fathers for Christian burial in nearby churches. The majority of the English dead were left to lie where they had fallen, strewn upon the ground, according to the *Carmen,* "to be devoured by worms and wolves, dogs and birds." Visiting the scene seventy years later, Ordericus Vitalis found their bones still lying on the ridge. The bodies of Aelfurg and his twelve monks were easily identified by the monastic garb they wore under their armor. The corpses of Gyrth and Leofwine were found, but the body of Harold could not be identified, despite the assistance of two monks from Waltham Abbey, Osgod and Aethelric, who had marched south with the King and had watched the battle from afar. A corpse, gashed with wounds and frightfully mutilated, was pulled from the pile of bodies lying around the standard. William had had to be certain that his rival was dead.

The story of the identification of Harold's body and its burial is shrouded in legend. According to one version, the monks from Waltham brought Godwine's widow, Gytha, to seek the bodies of her sons, and, when she failed to recognize Harold's, they fetched his ex-mistress, Edith of the Swan Neck, the mother of his three sons. She supposedly identified the mutilated body by secret marks known only to her. Gytha's offer to William to redeem her son's body by its weight in gold was tersely refused, and the Duke ordered William Malet to carry it to the seashore and bury it under a cairn of stones where, the Normans said in jest, the King could continue to guard the coast he had guarded with such insensate zeal in life. Later generations, however, found such a fate inadequate for their hero's body, and William of Malmesbury states that it was removed to Waltham Abbey, where it was buried with great honor in a tomb, which survived until the Abbey's dissolution in the sixteenth century.

The legend that Harold's body was finally accorded honorable burial was not enough for the myth-makers; within two centuries the story had become current that he had not been killed at Hastings. He was said to have been found half-dead by some women who took him secretly to his sister, the Confessor's widow, at Winchester where he was healed by a Saracen woman. Regaining his health, Harold journeyed throughout Europe, seeking allies with whom to regain his lost kingdom, finally reaching Chester, where he lived as a recluse in a monk's cell, disclosing his identity on his deathbed.

William had the satisfaction of gazing upon the dead body of his enemy, the perjurer who had stolen the kingdom that was his by right. He had killed the usurper King and routed his army. He had conquered England, but he did not yet know that. The English could raise another army; the two northern earls, Edwin and Morcar, could make him fight another battle for the throne. The brothers, it is said, were on their way south when they heard of King Harold's death. They sent their sister, Harold's widow, to Chester, where she is reported to have borne a son, and continued their march to London, where they conferred with Archbishop Stigand, Archbishop Eldred of York and the wounded Sheriff Esegar, who had to be carried on a litter. The crown was vacant; the enemy was at the gates. England required a king around whom the people could rally. The choice was limited. Harold's three young sons carried the stigma of illegitimacy. Edwin and Morcar tried to arrange, according to Florence of Worcester, that one or the other should be made king. They showed little enthusiasm for the Witan's choice, Edgar the Aetheling, the grandson of Edmund Ironside, who, as the date of his death (1125) suggests, must have been a child of not more than ten years of age, for they withdrew to the North in the belief, states William of Malmesbury, that William would never conquer that part of the island.

Duke William continued to be cautious. He returned to Hastings, where he tarried for five days, awaiting, says *The Anglo-Saxon Chronicle,* "whether the nation would submit to him," until he perceived that they would not come. The patrolling English fleet appears to have withdrawn, for the Duke was able to send to Normandy for reinforcements, which landed eventually at Bosham. Leaving Hastings in the charge of a brave commander, he moved eastward. A force was sent to take vengeance on the citizens of Romney, who had slain Normans, and the main army reached Dover on 21 October. The garrison of the castle offered clemency, surrendered, but castle and town were accidentally fired, to the anger of the Duke, who could not punish the offenders because there were too many. He recompensed the citizens. By his eastward march, William secured the seven major ports of southeast England, and it appears from the Domesday Survey, which records the ravages of the year, that he sent troops to seize the ports of Seaford, Shoreham and Bosham to the west. He thus secured his communications with Normandy and deprived the English fleet of its bases.

Still, the Normans did not march directly on London. They set out from Dover in a wide sweep to isolate the city. The line of their march is indicated by the devastations recorded in Domesday, which reduced the values of three hundred manors by one-third. Shortly after leaving Dover, the army was stricken with dysentery, and William himself succumbed at Canterbury, which caused a short delay, during which time he exchanged messages with Edith, the Confessor's widow, who was then at Winchester, who agreed to surrender the city. The army then moved on toward London, following the south bank of the Thames, ravaging and burning, until it reached the suburb of Southwark, where an English sortie across London Bridge was beaten back by the advance guard of five hundred knights. The army crossed the Thames fifty miles higher up at Wallingford on the Berkshire bank of the Thames, where Archbishop Stigand came to submit.

The Hon. Francis Baring (*Domesday Tables,* 1909) finds the event "fatal" to the Archbishop's reputation, for apparently he submitted to William two to three weeks before the general English surrender, which was made at Berkhamsted on 21 December. The wily Stigand, thinks Mr. Baring, deserted the failing cause, a supposition for which he deduces evidence from the record of Domesday, which shows that, although in the general devastation of Kent the Archbishop's personal property remained intact, his manor at Mortlake in Surrey was wasted. William tried to gain Stigand's allegiance by sparing his Kentish manors. When the Archbishop remained faithful to the Aetheling, the Duke put on pressure, which brought Stigand hurrying to change his allegiance. Mr. G. T. Turner ("William the Conqueror's March to London in 1066," *English Historical Review,* XXVII, 1912), on the other hand, finds Stigand's betrayal of the English cause less sinister. He came to prepare the way for the general surrender. William of Poitiers especially mentions that Stigand acted in concert with Edwin and Morcar, and the Archbishop's surrender is the only incident of the march he mentions, which suggests its supreme importance. The two northern earls were the chief obstacles to William's success, and they were the foes whose submission he most desired. The way for their surrender on the best possible terms was paved by Stigand, who arranged for them to come to Berkhamsted, which lay close to their road from Chester, along Watling Street and Upper Icknield Way.

The Duke's itinerary from Wallingford supports this supposition. Instead of turning on London, he marched fifty miles to the west, to meet the northern earls, perhaps at the manor of Monks Risborough which had been owned by the late Sheriff Esegar, and which lay between Wallingford and Berkhamsted. According to Guy of Amiens, Esegar, who was the military commander of London, had been in secret communication with William.

Whatever was the truth behind these obscure negotiations, the English magnates came to submit at Berkhampstead in Hertfordshire, bringing the Aetheling Edgar with them. There the two archbishops, Stigand and Eldred, Bishop Wulfstan of Worcester and Bishop Walter of Hereford, the chief men of London and the two northern earls begged William to accept England's vacant crown, and they offered him their fealty. The Duke received them graciously, and he accorded Edgar the kiss of peace. But to the offer of the throne, he demurred. He was reluctant to take the crown, he told his Norman friends, while the country still remained unsettled and so much resistance remained to be crushed. Besides, he wished to be crowned with his wife Matilda. It seemed foolish, therefore, to show undue haste in reaching for the peak of achievement.

William was being astute. He realized that the change of status from duke to king stirred a complex of loyalties. Anxious as were his barons that he should push the conquest of England to its logical conclusion, some, observes Professor Douglas (*William the Conqueror,* 1964), "were doubtless apprehensive lest William as king might be able unduly to enlarge in Normandy the rights which he already exercised as duke." William thought it prudent to display some hesitation, and it is perhaps significant, remarks Professor Douglas, "that in the debate which ensued the most strenuous argument in favour of an immediate Coronation was made not by a Norman magnate but by a Poitevin, Haimo, *vicomte* of Thouars."

William of Poitiers, who mistakes the place of English submission as occurring at Barking, tells us that Haimo (who had eulogized the Duke on Blackhorse Hill) was as famous for his speech as for his strong right arm. It was the fervent desire of the army that William should accept the throne, he told the Duke. William replied that he yielded to their wishes in the hope that, after he had begun to reign, men would hesitate to rebel against him or that, if they did so, they would be more easily crushed.

After he had formally accepted the crown, William advanced on London as king-elect. Still, apparently, some opposition flickered, for there are hints of skirmishes at Barking and Westminster. William himself waited on the outskirts of the city, sending his men forward to construct a fortress, the future Tower of London, and to make suitable preparations for his coming in royal splendor and for his coronation, which he ordered to be celebrated at Westminster Abbey on 25 December, Christmas Day. His crowning, he commanded, was to be conducted by Eldred, Archbishop of York, whom William of Poitiers describes as "a man equally esteemed for his holy life and spotless reputation," in contrast to Stigand, whom the Pope had stricken with anathema. The Archbishop of Canterbury was allowed to play only a minor part in the ceremony.

For the second time within a year the magnates of England gathered to exchange their reciprocal promises of rights and duties with their king-elect. This time the Abbey was crowded by Normans, and Norman soldiers guarded its doors. There were other subtle changes. William was King of England by right of conquest, a fact he was at pains to disguise. He made every effort to stress the continuity of royal rule. He was the inheritor of an unbroken royal succession, the legitimate successor of Edward the Confessor after an interim caused by usurpation. Hc cmphatically asserted his hereditary right to the throne on the expressed principles of Anglo-Saxon kingship; the late King had nominated him as his heir, and he had been elected by the magnates of England. Nonetheless, he was king by "right of blood"; he belonged to the English royal family through the marriage of his great-aunt Emma, sister of Duke Richard II and mother of Edward the Confessor. Now he came to seek God's blessing by sacramental unction, a ceremony particularly important to William, for the change of dynasty was thereby formally legitimized by one of the most sacred rites of the Church, signifying the acceptance of his fitness to rule by the authority of God.

The ceremony of William's coronation as King of the Angles and Saxons followed the traditional ordo of his predecessors, with a few changes. The usual reference to the King's father was inappropriate; the words "by hereditary right" were inserted instead. The litany was augmented by the inclusion of the *Laudes Regiae* from France, in which William was accorded the same salutation as was offered in Europe only to the Emperor and the King of France. Another innovation was necessary. Half the congregation spoke French; the vital parts of the ceremony were spoken in two languages. When it came to the customary acclamation of the new king by the assembled people, the questions were put by Archbishop Eldred in English and by the Bishop of Coutances in French. To their question, "Will you have this prince to be your king?" the two races shouted "yea" and "oui" with loud voices.

The shout of acclamation rang through the Minster and penetrated its walls. To the Norman guards, unaccustomed to a coronation, it sounded like a riot. Believing that a revolt had broken out, they set fire to the adjacent buildings and killed the bystanders. Hearing the roar of the flames and the cries of the English, the congregation rushed from the Abbey, some, according to Ordericus Vitalis, hoping to save their goods, others seeking plunder, leaving the king-elect and the officiating prelates standing alone at the altar. The rest of the ceremony was enacted in lonely splendor. King William was invested with the royal regalia, crowned and anointed with the holy oil in the absence of his new subjects, amid the uproar of death and destruction. Few people heard his solemn promise to rule as well as the best of kings who had gone before him.

The ceremony finished, the bishops conducted William to the Abbey's west door, where he mounted his horse to ride the few hundred yards to his palace by the Thames to begin his reign as King William of England, no longer William the Bastard. The world had accorded William the title of Conqueror. It signified his unique achievement. His conquest was permanent.

Fifteen

The Adventurers

The Norman conquest of England looked anything but permanent as the momentous year 1066 drew to its close. Duke William had scaled the drainpipe, climbed into the house, slain the landlord and seized his goods. He was the richest prince in Europe. But the hardest part of his job lay ahead. He was like the beast of prey prowling the jungle with a hunk of bleeding flesh in his mouth, his greedy rivals licking their jaws and snapping curs at his heels. William had now to reward his followers and protect his loot. He spent the remainder of his days defending his Anglo-Norman kingdom. The task gave him no respite for twenty-one years.

On 5 January, 1067, the anniversary of the death of his "predecessor," as William considered his cousin Edward, prospects for the peaceful settlement of England seemed good. William had subjugated the southern half, and the North had submitted to him. Most of the ancient nobility had been killed in the three great battles of the preceding year. To the survivors he offered a share of the kingdom. He confirmed Edwin and Morcar in their earldoms, created a new earldom from the shires of Huntingdon, Northampton, Bedford and Cambridge and bestowed it upon Siward's son Waltheof. He kept the Aetheling at his side, and he ignored Stigand's equivocal position as schismatic Archbishop of Canterbury. To satisfy the immediate claims of the barons of Normandy, France and Brittany, he confiscated the estates of the men "who stood against me in battle and were slain there," and handed them out as the first spoils of war. But he did not give any fiefs in absolute ownership; each parcel of land carried its obligations of military service. William thus created the force with which he defended his realm, an aristocracy designed for war.

The English and the Normans settled down in peaceful amity. By his statesmanship William had satisfied both races. The Norman barons took over the estates of their "ancestors," as the deceased owners were called to emphasize William's legal claim to the throne, and some married English wives. They even adopted the English fashions of long hair and pointed toes. The surviving English nobles and prelates ruled their earldoms and estates as before. Nothing was changed. Each Norman, French and Breton landowner was ordered to accept the rights and obligations of his predecessor, and William retained the royal administrative system and the laws and customs of old England. He made one change only. The writs issued by the King's writing office were no longer phrased in Anglo-Saxon. They were written in monkish Latin.

By March the pacification of England seemed so complete that William deemed it safe to return to Normandy, leaving the kingdom in the care of his two half-brothers and his seneschal, William Fitz-Osbern. As a precaution, he took with him those English leaders around whom the disaffected might rally. Edwin, Morcar, the Aetheling, Stigand and other bishops joined as honored guests the party that sailed from Pevensey in the fleet, the sails of which had been changed to white to denote triumph and victory. William was accorded a great reception in Normandy; his people were astonished by the display of England's wealth in gold and jewels and by the presence of his gilded prisoners. He confirmed the grants of land he had promised to the great religious foundations, among them the Abbey of Jumièges which received the whole of Hayling Island, off the Hampshire coast (where I am writing this book). The frontiers of Normandy were quiet. The King of France was still a minor, secure under the guardianship of Baldwin V of Flanders, William's father-in-law. In December the Duke-King returned to England.

The appearance of tranquility was deceptive; the English rose in revolt. From 1068 to 1073 William faced almost continual crises; sporadic rebellions flared. The Welsh, the Scots and Harold's three sons, who had taken refuge in Ireland, raided; the Danes invaded. William met violence with violence. The ferocity of his vengeance probably reflected his disappointment at the failure of his scheme to unify the English and the Normans. The English rebelled against strong centralized rule; each earl and thegn wished to retain his freedom to plunder and despoil his neighbors, as he had done for centuries and as the Norman barons had tried to do before William curbed them. There was no national rising against King William, no concerted action; the rebellions were confused and incoherent. When Exeter and the West rose, Yorkshire remained quiet. When York revolted, the West stood aloof. When the Danes invaded, their northern compatriots discussed rebellion; the Danes had been driven off before the English had made up their minds. William's energy was phenomenal; the system of feudal obligation supplied him with a force of four thousand mounted knights. He dashed to the west, to the north, building strong points to overawe the countryside, harrying, laying waste. To those who submitted, he was magnanimous. When Eustace of Boulogne sought to gain personal advantage from the worsening situation, William forgave him. Eustace had crossed the Channel and besieged Dover, but its garrison had chased him ignominiously back across the sea.

By the summer of 1069 William was in effective control of all England south of the Humber. Then King Sweyn of Denmark came again, this time with a fleet of 240 ships, an invasion almost as great as that of Harald Hardrada. Earl Waltheof, who had been placed in his earldom to defend England against the Danes, joined his Scandinavian cousins. William rushed to the North, savagely devastating the land; his harrying was so systematic and brutal that its effects were still evident twenty years later. The Domesday Survey records "waste" by the name of manor after manor. In midwinter, William led his troops, mutinous from the hardships of the march, across the Pennine hills to Chester. Waltheof was captured and executed.

The Danes sailed away. When they returned in 1070, the East Anglians rose in revolt. Their leader, Hereward, called the Wake, sacked Peterborough and withdrew to the Isle of Ely, deep in the Fen country, where he was joined by Earl Morcar. Edwin was murdered by his own followers. William bought off the Danes and besieged Ely. Morcar was taken prisoner and transferred to Normandy, where he eventually died. Hereward escaped to become the legendary spirit of native resistance against the rule of an alien race. Two years later William led his knights on a punitive expedition to Scotland, where he forced King Malcolm to pay him homage.

The worst was over. England had been pacified. The native aristocracy lost everything in its senseless opposition. Its estates were forfeited to the crown. Up to 1069 two-thirds of England had been ruled by men of English birth and parentage; in 1086 only two Englishmen are recorded as holding estates of baronial dimensions, and only eight percent of the land remained in English possession. The destruction of old England was complete; William had created a new system.

The term "feudalism" is now a dirty word, one that signifies the imagined evils deriving from the system the Normans imposed to defend their English realm. By it, they created an aristocracy, which, in return for land, rendered military service when summoned. Whether William founded feudalism in England or found a similiar system already in being (the controversy is unending), he adapted Norman ideas to the peculiar conditions of his new kingdom. Feudalism enabled him to satisfy the desires of his followers for wealth and power and, at the same time, to prevent them from abusing their strength. He needed a permanent military force, which was provided by the great barons and prelates, each of whom was required to put into the field a specified number of knights, the *servitium debitum,* as it was called. To achieve this, William divided England into great baronial fiefs. He retained a quarter of the land himself, gave another quarter to the Church and divided the remainder among 180 tenants-in-chief. To provide the service required from them, these chief tenants, lay and ecclesiastical, enfeoffed their knights, granting them land, which gave each knight the wealth with which to equip himself and to fulfill his obligations. Sir Charles Oman says:

> the eleventh-century knight was not necessarily nobly born, nor had he gone through the elaborate ceremony of admission to the knightly order which prevailed three centuries later. He was simply a soldier who fought on horseback, and who received from the king, or from one of the king's tenants-in-chief, a patch of land on condition that he should do mounted service in return for it.

William capped this pyramid of contractual land tenure by extracting, at Salisbury, an oath of allegiance from every baron and each influential knight, directly to him as sovereign, over and above the loyalty each man owed his immediate overlord, a far more sophisticated system than that he had inherited in Normandy, where the feudal system relied on a crazy patchwork of loyalties and obligations, in which no direct oath to the Duke was required. In Normandy, Duke William had been unable to prevent the knights from supporting their lords' private feuds. In England, where he established feudalism by arbitrary act, William outlawed private war. He also vastly increased the service owed by the great barons for their estates in England over the service the same men owed in Normandy, and he concentrated his power by allocating the majority of English land to the dominant inner circle of his own relatives and friends, the men who had grown up with him and had supported him from his youth. To the ordinary knight, he gave a stake in the community, thus ensuring his loyalty and good behavior.

William's half-brothers, Eude of Bayeux and Robert of Mortain, became the most powerful men in England, each holding vast estates spread throughout the country. Everyone who had helped William win the crown was rewarded. The mercenaries were paid from the wealth derived from England's taxation, which brought William revenues far surpassing those of any contemporary European ruler. The gloomy Fitz-Wymarc was rewarded with the Earldom of East Anglia. Alan Fergant, who had led the Breton contingent, was created Earl of Richmond in Yorkshire, and the pusillanimous and treacherous Eustace of Boulogne was granted great estates, which he passed on to his two sons, one of whom, Godfrey, became in time the first crusading King of Jerusalem. Nor did William forget his promise to the monks of Marmoutier.

After the conquest was complete, William sent William Faber to Marmoutier to bring monks to build the great abbey he had vowed to found on the spot where God had given him victory. When the monks examined the ridge, they judged it unsuitable for the great foundation and commenced their building on its western slopes, nearer to the water they considered essential. William was furious. He ordered them to start again exactly where he had commanded. The abbey was not completed until the next reign, and it was dedicated to St. Martin in 1094. Its buildings survived until the dissolution of the monasteries in the sixteenth century, when they were rebuilt as a private dwelling, which now accommodates a private school for girls.

Four years elapsed before William could reward Lanfranc with the See of Canterbury. In 1070 the Pope sent an ecclesiastical commission to England, led by Ermenfrid, Bishop of Sitten. After an inquiry, he deposed Stigand, who was accused of the crime of holding two bishoprics, Winchester and Canterbury, at the same time. He retired to his private estates, accusing William of bad faith, and died two years later.

Hildebrand became pope in 1073, taking the name of Gregory VII. Six years later, when he was at the height of his power, with the Emperor grovelling at his feet, Hildebrand presented the bill for his support of William's cause, which had brought him so much calumny in the papal court. William, he claimed, had promised to recognize St. Peter as his suzerain, to subordinate temporal authority to the spiritual control of Rome. He invited King William to pay his debt. William tersely refused. "I had not consented to pay fealty," he told the Pope, "Nor will I now, because I never promised it, nor do I find that my predecessors ever paid it to your predecessors." He sent the Pope instead Harold's personal standard, the emblem of the fighting man. Two years later Gregory was deposed by a schismatic rival, and he died in exile in 1085.

The conquest of England had been achieved by the shedding of much Christian blood, which was deplored, if not by Hildebrand, at least by the papal curia. In 1070 the Church gave its absolution, announced by Bishop Ermenfrid. He imposed a set of penances on all ranks of the victorious army. Every man who had fought at Hastings was required to do a year's penance for each man whom he had killed. If he could not tell the number, he was allowed to commute the penance by gifts to the Church. The mercenary soldiers were required to do penance as for homicide, and the archers were ordered to observe a triple Lent. Similar penances were exacted for killings done after the battle; a year's penance was appointed for the death of a man killed while resisting the seizure of food, three years for the death of a man resisting wanton plunder. Everyone was satisfied; the Church had salved its conscience, and the soldiers were absolved for their deeds of blood.

With these matters settled and England pacified, William could turn his attention to Normandy, where a serious situation was developing. The hostile confederations that William had faced and overcome before the Conquest had been revived. Baldwin V of Flanders had died in 1067, and Philip of France had grown up. He set out to separate Normandy from England. Throughout the remainder of William's life, the King of France supported his enemies, inciting and encouraging the revolt of William's own son Robert, who had the temerity to defeat his father in battle. Everywhere the Norman frontiers were threatened; Flanders was hostile, Maine in revolt, Anjou unified and dangerous once more, the Bretons rebellious. William plunged into a turmoil of war to protect his heritage. To defend his frontiers he brought contingents of the English fyrd across the Channel. They fought alongside his barons and their knights.

The Normans had learned the value of infantry from their near-defeat at Hastings. The victory had been accepted by all of Europe as convincing proof of the superiority of cavalry over foot soldiers. The Normans knew better. It is significant for the true assessment of the Battle of Hastings that, in the next 75 years, the Anglo-Normans dismounted their knights to fight at Tinchebrai in 1106, at Brémule in 1119, at the Battle of the Standard in 1138 and again at Lincoln in 1141. The chivalry of France clung to its horses and went down to terrible defeat at Crécy in 1346. The Anglo-Normans were the first warlike race to appreciate the solidarity of well-armed, disciplined infantry used in conjunction with cavalry, a tactic incomprehensible to the Continental baronial class, which held infantry in contempt. These barons tried to persuade the Pope to ban the use of crossbows, whose bolts penetrated their armor. The papal anathema directed against this class-leveling weapon proved ineffective, and the English longbow, which had a higher rate of fire than the crossbow, became the master weapon of the medieval battlefield and, with gunpowder, the downfall of the mounted knight.

To defend his Norman frontiers and consolidate his kingdom, William needed to know precisely the military strength and taxable capacity of England. To discover these facts he instituted what has been called by Sir Frank Stenton (*Anglo-Saxon England,* 1962) an administrative achievement without parallel in medieval history, the Domesday

Survey. William set the inquiry in motion by a "very deep speech" delivered to his council, which was assembled at Gloucester in 1085. He wished to learn, he stated, how England was peopled and with what sort of men. *The Anglo-Saxon Chronicle* describes the king's inquiry thus:

> He sent his men over all England into every shire and had them find out how many hundred hides there were in the shire, or what land and cattle the king himself had in the country, or what dues he ought to have annually from the shire. Also, he had a record made of how much land his archbishops had, and his bishops and his abbots and his earls—and though I related at too great length—what or how much everybody had who was occupying land in England, in land and cattle, and how much money it was worth. So very narrowly did he have it investigated that there was no single hide nor a yard of land nor indeed (shame it is to relate it but it seemed no shame to him to do) was one ox or one cow or one pig left out, that was not put down in his record. And all these writings were brought to him afterwards.

The great inquest was highly unpopular, and it led to violence. The English recognized its fiscal nature by naming it Domesday.

William's last years were spent, as had been his youth, in peril and adversity. Queen Matilda died in 1083 (the opening of her coffin in 1961 disclosed the bones of a woman of diminutive size, little more than four feet tall), and his half-brother Eude became disaffected and had to be imprisoned. William was sixty years of age, becoming heavy and corpulent, a condition that contributed to his death in 1087. Campaigning in the Vexin, a territory disputed with France, he rode through the burning streets of Mantes. His horse took fright, and he was thrown against the pommel, sustaining injuries from which he died at Rouen on 9 September. As was the custom, his eldest son Robert succeeded to his dukedom, the inherited lands, while his second son William Rufus became King of England, the land won by conquest. The third son Henry took the cash, and eventually he reunited the dukedom and the kingdom.

William and his Normans founded a new race—the English. They drew old England away from her Germanic and Scandinavian past and oriented her toward France and Italy, where she absorbed the culture of the Latins, to her inestimable gain. They brought other blessings. The Normans were astute politicians; their descendants have become the most politically mature nation on earth. The Normans had many rare qualities, the greatest perhaps being their capacity for improvisation and adaptation; for nine centuries the English have shown their capacity to adapt themselves to changed conditions, never so successfully as during the great and almost unnoticed revolution that started in 1945. The Normans in their day were unloved; the English have gained the respect but not the affection of their neighbors. The Normans were adventurers, ready, says Ordericus Vitalis, "for every wild adventure." English history is filled with mad adventures, as hazardous and as successful as the Norman invasion of England. The Normans calculated the risks and attended to every detail, gaining thereby a dramatic victory at Hastings, which Sir Frank Stenton describes as one of those battles that "at rare intervals have decided the fate of nations."

Appendix

A.

The Conqueror's Companions

Some seven to ten thousand men accompanied Duke William across the English Channel in September 1066. Others came from Normandy afterward, and several Normans are known to have been resident in England before the Conquest. The names of few men, who fought at Hastings, are established with certainty, for they appear in the best respected contemporary authorities. The names of another three hundred rest on circumstantial evidence.

Professor David Douglas, who has discussed the question in *History,* Vol. XXVIII (1943), lists 32 names vouched for by evidence deduced from the Bayeux Tapestry, William of Poitiers, Guy of Amiens, Ordericus Vitalis and various Norman charters:

Eustace, Count of Boulogne
Robert, Count of Mortain
William, son of Richard, Count of Evreux
Geoffrey, son of Rotrou, Count of Mortagne
Eude, Bishop of Bayeux
Geoffrey, Bishop of Coutances
William Fitz-Osbern
Aimeri, Vicomte of Thouars
Walter Giffard
Ralf de Tosny

Hugh de Montfort
Hugh de Grandmesnil
William de Warenne
Robert, son of Roger de Beaumont
William Malet
Guilbert d'Auffay
Robert de Vitot
Engenulf de Laigle
Gerelmus de Panileuse
Robert Fitz-Erneis
Roger, son of Turold
Turstin, son of Rollo
Erchembald, son of Erchembald the Vicomte
Vitalis
Wadard
Taillefer
A member of the house of Ponthieu (perhaps Count Guy I)
Gerald the Seneschal
Rodulf the Chamberlain (of Tancarville)
Hugh d'Ivry, the Butler
Richard Fitz-Gilbert
Pons

Two other "lists" have been compiled. In 1866, a roll of names was drawn up by a committee of French scholars, and three years later 485 names were inscribed on the west wall of the church at Dives, where the Conqueror and his companions heard mass before embarking. In 1931, 315 names compiled by Professors M. Jackson Crispin (Princeton University) and Léonce Macary (Collège of Falaise), were inscribed on a bronze tablet which was placed in the chapel of the château at Falaise. For these 315 names, in the view of those scholars, "strong presumption" exists.

Both rolls are based on the recognized sources, on Domesday Book and the best respected copies of Battle Abbey Roll. Clearly, the Domesday Survey, which recorded the owners of land in England in 1086, is no certain guide as to whether or not those men "came over with the Conqueror," for some may have been their sons, or they may have crossed the Channel before or after 1066. Conversely, the omission of a name from Domesday does not prove that a man did not fight at Hastings, for many of the Conqueror's followers were not rewarded with land in England.

Battle Abbey Roll, which may have been based on the list recorded at Dives and which may have been read after the battle to ascertain who was alive and who was dead, disappeared in the fourteenth century. It is known only in copies, of which the best respected are those made by Holinshed and Leland.

As the more modern of the two lists, the Falaise Roll commands the greatest authority for the presumption of names other than those founded on direct evidence. It records these names:

FALAISE ROLL

Adam de Rie
Achard d'Ambrieres
Amaury, Vicomte de Thouars
Alain Fergant, Comte de Bretagne
Alain Fitz Flaald
Le Comte Alain Le Noir
Le Comte Alain Le Roux
Alric Le Coq
André de Vitrie
Anscoul de Picquigni
Ansger de Montaigu
Anquetil de Ros
Ansgot de Ros
Arnoul d'Ardre
Aubri de Couci
Auvrai le Breton
Auvrecher d'Angerville
Avenel des Biards
Le Sire d'Argouges
Le Sire d'Anisy
Le Sire d'Aubigny (Roger)
Le Sire d'Auvillers
Baudoin de Meules et du Sap
Berenger Giffard
Bernard de Neufmarché
Bernard de St-Ouen
Bernard de St-Valéry
Bertran de Verdun
Le Sire de Bailleul
Le Sire de Beville et d'Yvelin
Le Sire de Bolleville
Le Sire de Bonnebosq
Le Sire de Bosc-Roard
Le Sire de Bouttevillain
Le Seigneur de Brecey
Le Sire de Brucourt
Corbet Le Normand
Le Sire de Canouville
Le Sire de Cintheaux
Le Sire de Clinchamps
Le Sire de Couvert
Le Sire de Cussy
Dreu de La Beuvriêre
Dreu de Montaigu
Durand Malet
Le Sire de Driencourt
Engenoulf de l'Aigle
Errand de Harcourt
Etienne Erard
Eudes, Evêque de Bayeux
Eudes, Comte de Champagne
Eudes Dapifer, Sire de Préaux
Eudes de Fourneaux
Eudes Le Seneschal, Sire de la Haie
Eustache, Comte de Boulogne
Le Sire d'Epinay
Le Sire d'Escalles
Fouque d'Aulnay
Fouque d'Aunou
Le Sire de Fribois
Gautier d'Aincourt
Gautier d'Appeville
Gautier de Caen
Gautier Le Flamand
Gautier Giffard, Comte de Longueville
Gautier Hachet
Gautier de Lacy
Gautier Le Poitevin
Gautier de Vernon
Geoffroi Ascelin
Geoffroi du Bec
Geoffroi de Combray
Geoffroi, Evêque de Coutances
Geoffroi de la Guierche
Geoffroi de Mandeville
Geoffroi, Seigneur de Mortagne
Geoffroi Martel
Geoffroi de Pierrepont
Geoffroi Ridel
Geoffroi Talbot
Gilbert d'Asnières
Gilbert Le Blond
Gilbert de Bretteville
Gilbert de Colleville
Gilbert Crispin 2e Seigneur de Tillières
Gilbert de Gand
Gilbert Malet
Gilbert de Neuville
Gilbert Tison
Gilbert de Venables
Giles de Picquigni
Gonfroi de Cioches
Gui de la Val
Guilbert d'Aufay
Guillaume Alis
Guillaume d'Alre
Guillaume d'Anneville
Guillaume L'Archer
Guillaume d'Arques
Guillaume d'Audrieu
Guillaume Bacon, Sire du Molay
Guillaume de Beaufou
Guillaume Bertram
Guillaume Le Blond
Guillaume du Bosc
Guillaume de Bourneville
Guillaume de Brai
Guillaume de Briouse
Guillaume de Cahaignes

Guillaume de Cailly
Guillaume La Chièvre
Guillaume de Colleville
Guillaume de Colombieres
Guillaume Crispin 1re Comte du Vexin
Guillaume Bigot
Guillaume de Gouvix
Guillaume Comte d'Evreux
Guillaume de Ferrières
Guillaume Fitz Osberne
Guillaume de Lacelles
Guillaume Louvet
Guillaume Malet de Graville
Guillaume de La Mare
Guillaume de Monceaux
Guillaume de Moulins S. de Falaise
Guillaume de Moyon
Guillaume de St-Jean
Guillaume de Pantoul
Guillaume Patry, de la Lande
Guillaume Pêché
Guillaume de Percy
Guillaume Pevrel
Guillaume de Picquigni
Guillaume Le Poitevin
Guillaume de Reviers
Guillaume de Ros
Guillaume de Roumare
Guillaume Saye
Guillaume de Semilly
Guillaume Taillebois
Guillaume Talbot
Guillaume de Toeni
Guillaume de Vieuxpont
Guillaume de Warren
Godefroi de Villers
Guineboud de Balon
Le Sire de Gacé
Le Sire de Glanville
Le Sire de Glos
Hamelin de Balon
Hamon de la Val
Hamon Le Seneschal
Hascouf Musard
Henri de Domfront
Henri de Ferrières
Herbert d'Aigneaux
Honfroi de Bohon
Honfroi de Carteret
Honfroi Vis de Loup
Huard de Vernon
Hubert de Port
Hubert de Rie
Hugue L'Asne
Hugue de Beauchamp
Hugue de Bernières
Hugue de Bolbec
Hugue de Carbonnel
Hugue de Gournay
Hugue de Gournay "Le Jeune"
Hugue de Grentemesnil
Hugue de Macey
Hugue de La Mare
Hugue de Montfort le Connestable
Hugue de Mortemer
Hugue Musard
Hugue de Port
Hugue de Roussel
Hugue de St-Quentin
Hugue de Wanci
Hugue d'Héricy
Hugue d'Houdetot
Ibert de Lacy
Ingelram de Lions
Ive Taillebois
Ive de Vassy
Jacques le Brabançon
Jean d'Ivri
Le Sire de Jort
Le Sire de Lithaire
Martin de Tours
De Muscamp
Mathieu de la Ferté Macé
Mauger de Carteret
Michel de Bures
Mile Crispin
De Mathan
Du Merle
Néel Vicomte de St-Sauveur
Osberne d'Arques
Osberne de Sassy
Osberne Giffard
Osberne de Wanci
Osmond Basset
Ours d'Abbetot
Le Sire d'Origny
Le Sire d'Orglande
Paisnel des Moutiers-Hubert
Picot de Saye
Le Sire de Pacy
Le Sire des Pins
Le Chevalier de Pirou
Le Sire de Poer
Le Sire de Praères
Raoul Basset
Raoul Botin
Raoul L'Estourmi
Raoul de Fougères
Raoul de Gaël
Raoul Lambert
Raoul de Limesi
Raoul de Malherbe
Raoul de Mortemer
Raoul d'Ouilli
Raoul de La Pommeraie
Raoul de Sassy
Raoul de Rie
Raoul Taillebois
Raoul Tesson
Raoul de Tilly
Raoul de Toeni, Sieg. d'Acquigny
Raoul Le Veneur
Richard, Vicomte d'Avranches
Richard de Beaumais
Richard de Bienfaite et d'Orbec
Richard de Courci
Richard L'Estourmi
Richard de Neuville
Richard de Reviers
Richard de St-Clair

Richard de Sourdeval
Richard Talbot
Richard de Vernon
Robert d'Amfreville
Robert Banastre
Robert Le Bastard
Robert de Beaufou
Robert de Beaumont
Robert Bertram, le Tort
Robert Blouet
Robert Bourdet
Robert de Brix
Robert de Buci
Robert de Comines
Robert de Chandos
Robert de Coignieres
Robert de Courson
Robert Le Despensier
Robert Comte d'Eu
Robert de Crévecœur
Robert d'Estouteville
Robert Fitz-Erneis
Robert Guernon Sire de Montfiquet
Robert de Harcourt
Robert Malet
Robert Marmion de Fontenai
Robert Moreton
Robert Murdac
Robert Comte de Mortain
Robert d'Ouilli
Robert de Pierrepont
Robert de St-Léger
Robert de Toeni
Robert de Vassy
Robert de Vaux
Roger d'Abernon
Roger Arundel
Roger Bigot Sieg. de Maltot
Roger de Breteuil
Roger d'Amondeville
Roger Daniel
Roger d'Evreux
Roger de Montbray
Roger de Montgomeri
Roger Moreton
Roger de Mussegros
Roger d'Oistreham
Roger Picot
Roger Le Poitevin
Roger de Rames
Roger de St-Germain
Serion de Burci
Simon de Senlis
Le Sire de Rebercil
Le Sire de Rupierre
Le Sire de St-Martin
Le Sire de St-Sever
Le Sire de Soligny
Taillefer
Thierri Pointel
Toustain Basset
Toustain Fitz-Rou
Turold
Le Chamberlain de Tancarville
Le Sire de Touchet
Le Sire de Touques
Le Sire de Tournebut
Le Sire de Tourneur
Le Sire de Tourneville
Le Sire de Tracy
Le Sire de Tregoz
Le Sire de Troussebot
De Venois
Le Sire de Vesli (Honfroi)
Vital
Wadard

ADDITIONAL NAMES ACCEPTED

Adam de Brix
Adam Fitz Durand
Adelolfus de Mert
Aitard de Vaux
Amfroi de Condé
Anchetil de Grai
Anscelin Goël de Percival
Ansfroi de Vaubadon
Ansger de Criquetot
Ansold de Maule
Aubrai de Ver
Auvrai d'Espagne
Auvrai de Lincoln
Auvrai Maubenc
Auvrai de Merleberge
Bagod d'Arras
Baudri de Limesi
Blundel
Brient de Bretagne, Comte de Vannes
David d'Argentan
Enisand Musard
Eudes Fitz Spirwic
Fitz Bertran de Peleit
Fulcher de Maloure
Garnier de Senlis
Gautier du Bec
Gautier Le Ewrus
Gautier de Doui
Gautier Fitz Autier
Gautier de Saint-Valéry
Germond de Saint-Ouen
Gilbert de Montfichet
Goisfrid de Ros
Guarin de Maule
Gui, Comte de Ponthieu
Gui de Craon
Guido de Saint-Maur
Guillaume d'Aubigny 1er
Guillaume de l'Aune
Guillaume de Brix
Guillaume Corbon
Guillaume Maubenc
Guillaume de Valecherville
Guillaume de Vatteville
Hamon de Clervaux
Hervé de Bourges
Hervé d'Espagne
Hervé d'Hélion
Hubert Heusé
Hubert de Rie "le Jeune"
Hugue Bourdet

Hugue Le Boutellier
Hugue Corbon
Hugue de Guidville
Hugue de Vesly
Juhel de Mayenne
Maurin de Caen
Mile de Vesly
Néel de Monneville
Néel de Toeni
Noël
Norman D'Arcy
Raoul d'Asnières
Raoul de Beaufou
Raoul de Branche
Raoul Painel
Renaud de Vautort
Renouf Pevrel
Renouf de Saint-Valéry
Richard de l'Aigle
Richard d'Engagne
Robert L'Archer
Robert d'Armentières
Robert Bigot
Robert Le Blond
Robert de Breherval
Robert Fitz Picot
Robert Fitz Richard
Robert de Grenville
Robert de Todeni
Robert de Vesly
Robert de Vitot
Robert de Vitrie
Robert de Vieuxpont
Roger de Courcelles
Roger d'Ivri
Ruaud l'Aboube (Musard)
Serlon de Ros
Tihel de Héron
Le Sire de Tournièr
Turchil Le Roux

Readers will note the inclusion of the name of Eudes de Fourneaux (which occurs also in the Dives Roll). His name is found in the best-respected copies of the Battle Abbey Roll, and he is recorded in Domesday as holding half a hide of land as a tenant-in-chief in the County of Somerset in 1083. Another of the name, Anguetil, is recorded as holding lands in Yorkshire and Norfolk, and Ordericus Vitalis refers to Ralph de Fourneaux as witnessing a charter at St. Evrout in Normandy in 1070. Two villages, Fourneaux-sur-Vire, near Saint Lô, Manche, and Fourneaux-le-Val, close to Falaise, exist still.

Whether or not Eudes fought at Hastings cannot be established with certainty, but the early date of his land grant suggests that he was rewarded for his services in 1066. The name continues in western and eastern counties, and several members of the family achieved local prominence as knights of the shire and sheriffs of the county. Three villages in England carry the name, Ainderby Furneaux in Yorkshire, Furneaux Pelham in Hertfordshire and Pury Furneaux in Somerset.

No one alive today can establish direct descent, by legal process, from a companion of the Conqueror. Registration of birth, marriage and death did not become compulsory until 1533, and up to then, except perhaps in the case of people nationally prominent, the only records were those of ownership of land and summoning to military service. Nonetheless, many people living in Britain, the Commonwealth and the United States can reasonably claim to belong to families that may have been founded in the eleventh century, especially if their names are the same as those then recorded. For example, my claim to be a descendant of Eudes de Fourneaux is based on the recorded presence for centuries of men of my surname living in the same districts and bearing the same Christian names and coat of arms until 1562, from which date my descent can be established by documentary record. As in many families, there is a break in continuity for some years after 1349, when two-thirds of the population was wiped out by the black death.

Discussion of descent from Norman ancestors can be found in L. G. Pine, *They Came with the Conqueror,* London, 1954.

B.

The Field of Hastings

Those who propose to inspect the battlefield are advised to obtain the pamphlet written by Lieutenant Colonel Charles H. Lemmon, D.S.O., late Royal Artillery, entitled *The Field of Hastings* (3rd edition, 1965), which may be purchased at the Battle Book Shop, High Street, Battle, Sussex. The weight of the pamphlet in an envelope is three ounces, and the price, in 1965, three shillings and six pence.

The battle ridge is partly covered by the buildings of Battle Abbey, by trees and, at its eastern end, by the southern extension of Battle High Street. The scene of the battle can be viewed from several points, which are listed on Colonel Lemmon's plan. The visitor can stand at the spot where King Harold fought and died, marked now by the foundations of the Abbey chapel, which were disclosed in 1817. At the western end of the terrace of the Abbey (to which the public is admitted), he can look down toward the famous "hillock," the ground around which is still boggy and treacherous, and toward the extremity of the ridge where the English right flank probably rested. The likely position of the east flank can be seen near the state school, close to where Marley Lane leads from the High Street. The Norman position can be studied from the slopes of Telham Hill, access to which can be gained by a footpath that leads from the Hastings road, about two hundred yards south of the garage. The best place from which to examine the battleground is the Battle-Bexhill road which runs westward through the valley, from the eastern end of which leads the farm track, following the line of the original road from Hastings northward. Visitors should not omit to climb Caldbec Hill, where, from close to the windmill, a panoramic view can be obtained, which includes the slopes to the north down which the Norman and French knights plunged to their doom in Malfosse, which itself is difficult to find without a knowledgeable local guide.

To the question, Have any relics of the battle been found? the answer is No, because of the rise in level of the ground (one foot per hundred years for untrodden ground) and the acidic nature of the soil, which has probably destroyed both bones and weapons. A small axe head, which appears to date from the eleventh century, has been found in Marley Lane.

C.

Sources, Authorities and Acknowledgments

Primary Sources in approximate chronological order:

Eleventh Century

The Bayeux Tapestry — Believed to have been worked in England to the order of Eude, Bishop of Bayeux, within twenty years of the events it records. It was probably made to be hung in Bayeux Cathedral (consecrated 1077). Stitched in eight colors of thread on coarse linen, it is 231⅛ feet (70.34 meters) long and 19⅛ inches (50 centimeters) wide. It depicts, with captions, the story of Harold's oath and its consequences. It illustrates the Battle of Hastings in remarkable detail, supplying information without which we should know little about eleventh-century warfare. It depicts 623 persons, 202 horses and mules, 55 dogs, 505 other animals, 37 buildings, 41 ships, and 49 trees—1,512 objects in all. It is exhibited in the old bishop's palace at Bayeux, with a recorded commentary in several languages.

Gesta Normannorum Ducum (The Acts of the Norman Dukes) — Written by William of Jumièges, who died in 1090 and who carries his narrative down to the year 1072. His information respecting the Conquest is scanty.

Gesta Guillelmi Ducis Normannorum et Regis Anglorum (The Acts of William, Duke of Normandy and King of the English)

Written shortly after 1071 by William of Poitiers. As the Duke's chaplain during the invasion of England, his work is authoritative and, with the Tapestry, the best contemporary source. It tells the story of the invasion from the Norman point of view, and it is both prejudiced and occasionally inaccurate. Originally a soldier, William became a priest and Archdeacon of Lisieux.

The Anglo-Saxon Chronicle

The most important English source narrative, covering the years before and after the Conquest in three versions and drawing on contemporary information. Its information about the Conquest is scanty.

Twelfth Century

Historia Ecclesiastica Angliae et Normandie (The Ecclesiastical History of England and Normandy)

By Ordericus Vitalis, born in England, who became a monk in Normandy. He visited Hastings about seventy years after the battle and wrote this work sometime before 1140.

Draco Normannicus (The Norman Dragon)

Ascribed to St. Etienne of Rouen and written about 1150.

The Chronicle of Battle Abbey

Written by the monks about 1150.

Roman de Rou et des Ducs de Normandie (The Romance of Rollo and of the dukes of Normandy).

By Robert Wace, written about 1160.

De Bello Hastingensis Carmen (The Song about the Battle of Hastings)

Attributed to Guy, Bishop of Amiens and written before 1070.

Chronique des Ducs de Normandie (Chronicle of the dukes of Normandy)

By Benoît de St. More, written about 1190.

Vita Edwardi Confessoris (Life of Edward the Confessor)	The date of this work is disputed, and it may be a product of the eleventh century.
Chronicon ex Chronicis (The Chronicle of Chronicles)	By Florence of Worcester, written before 1110.
Gesta Regum Anglorum (The Acts of the English Kings)	By William of Malmesbury, written about 1125.
Historia Anglorum (History of England)	By Henry of Huntingdon, written after 1200.
Thirteenth Century	
The Heimskringla (Sagas of the Norse Kings)	Compiled by Snorri Sturluson, who drew on ancient traditions.

Secondary Sources

English Historical Documents (General Editor, David C. Douglas, M.A., F.B.A.) 1953, contains relevant sections from *The Anglo-Saxon Chronicle,* Florence of Worcester, William of Jumièges, William of Poitiers, The Bayeux Tapestry (whole), Ordericus Vitalis and William of Malmesbury.

Snorri's account of the battle of Stamford Bridge is contained in *The Heimskringla* (S. Laing, translator, 1889), Vol. IV.

The Chronicle of Battle Abbey has been translated by M. A. Lower, 1851.

Wace's chronicle has been translated by Edgar Taylor, 1837.

Editions of other authorities:

Benoît, edited by Michel, Paris, 1836–43

Carmen, edited by H. Petrie (*Monumenta Historica Britannica*), 1848

Vita Edwardi, edited by F. Barlow, Edinburgh, 1962

Henry of Huntingdon, edited by T. Arnold, 1879

Domesday Book, edited by the Record Commission, 1783.

Authorities

The Bayeux Tapestry, William of Poitiers, *The Anglo-Saxon Chronicle* and Ordericus Vitalis are considered the best authorities for the Norman Conquest, of which Professor David Douglas (*William the Conqueror,*

1964) has said, "few periods of our history remain more the subject of controversy." Considerable argument revolves around the value of Wace, of whose writings I have made extensive use. He wrote about one hundred years after the event, relying upon oral tradition, which must have been of intense vitality. Born in Jersey, he was educated at Caen, and for nineteen years he was Canon of Bayeux Cathedral. His lively narrative may not be without blemish, but without it the story of the Conquest would be dull indeed. I rely on Wace for the intimate details he received, no more than the modern historian depends upon the reports of war correspondents, which add so much color to official despatches. Wace may err in matters of detail, though, to quote Sir Charles Oman, "on the whole he comparatively seldom clashes with earlier writers in such a way as to show himself absolutely wrong." Extensive use of Wace is, I think, permissible in a book designed for the general reader who, unlike the student and the scholar, is generally badly informed about what was a tremendous and exciting event to those who experienced it and who handed down their stories to their sons and grandsons.

Bibliography

Anderson, R. and R. C. *The Sailing Ship. London,* 1926.
Baring, F. H. "The Malfosse at the Battle of Hastings," English Historical Review, XXII (1907).
———. *Notes on the Battle of Hastings.* Hastings, 1906.
Bliss, A. J. "The Companions of the Conqueror." *Litera III.* Valeta (1956).
Brooke, Z. N. "Pope Gregory VII's Demand for Fealty from William the Conqueror," *English Historical Review,* XXVI (1911).
Brooks, F. W. *The Battle of Stamford Bridge.* York, 1956.
———. *The English Naval Forces 1199–1272.* London, 1932.
Burne, A. H. *The Battlefields of England.* London, 1951.
Chambers, R. W. *England Before the Norman Conquest.* London, 1926.
Chevallier, C. T. "Where was Malfosse? The End of the Battle of Hastings," *Transactions, Battle and District Historical Society,* 1953.
Corbett, W. J. "The Development of the Duchy of Normandy and the Norman Conquest," *Cambridge Mediaeval History,* Vol. V, Chapter XV, 1926.
———. "England from 954 to the Death of Edward the Confessor," *Cambridge Mediaeval History,* Vol. III, Chapter XV, 1926.
Douglas, D. C. "Companions of the Conqueror," *History* XXVIII (1943).
———. "Edward the Confessor, Duke William of Normandy and the English Succession," *English Historical Review,* LXVIII (1953).
———. *The Norman Conquest and British Historians.* Glascow, 1946.
———. *William the Conqueror.* London, 1964.

Douglas, D. C., and Greenaway, G. W. *English Historical Documents, 1042–1189*. London, 1953.

Fowke, F. R. *The Bayeux Tapestry*. London, 1898.

Freeman, E. A. *The Norman Conquest*. 5 vols. London, 1870–1879.

Fuller, J. F. C. *Decisive Battles of the Western World*. Vol. II. London, 1954.

George, R. H. "The Contribution of Flanders to the Conquest of England," *Revue belge de philologie et d'histoire,* V (1926).

Glover, R. "English Warfare in 1066," *English Historical Review,* LXVII (1952).

Grierson, P. "The Relations between England and Flanders Before the Norman Conquest," *Trans. Royal Ry. Historical Society* 4th Series, XXIII (1941).

———. "A Visit of Earl Harold to Flanders in 1056," *English Historical Review,* LI (1936).

Haskins, C. H. "England Under William the Conqueror," *American Historical Review,* XIV (1909).

———. "Knight Service in Normandy in Eleventh Century," *English Historical Review* XII (1907).

———. *Norman Institutions*. Cambridge, Mass., 1918.

———. *The Normans in European History*. New York, 1915.

Hollister, C. W. *Anglo-Saxon Military Institutions on the Eve of the Norman Conquest*. Oxford, 1962.

——— "The Norman Conquest and the Genesis of English Feudalism," *American Historical Review,* LXVI (1961).

James, E. R. "The Battle of Hastings," *Royal Engineers Journal,* January 1907.

Landstrom, B. *The Ship*. London, 1961.

Larson, L. M. *The King's Household in England Before the Norman Conquest*. Madison, Wisc., 1904.

Legge, J. W. "Three Coronation Orders," *Henry Bradshaw Society* Proceedings XIX (1891).

Lemmon, C. H. *The Field of Hastings*. St. Leonard's on Sea, 1957.

Lower, M. A. *The Battle of Hastings*. (Pamphlet of unknown date)

Loyn, H. R. *Anglo-Saxon England and the Norman Conquest*. London, 1962.

MacLagan, E. *The Bayeux Tapestry*. London, 1943.

Margary, I. D. *Roman Ways in the Weald*. London, 1948.

Maskell. *Ancient Liturgy of the Church of England*. London, 1882.

Oleson, T. J. "Edward the Confessor's Promise of the Throne to Duke

William of Normandy," *English Historical Review* LXXII (1957).
———. *The Witenagemot in the Reign of Edward the Confessor.* Toronto, 1955.

Oman, Sir C. *The Art of War in the Middle Ages.* 2 vols. London, 1924.

Prestwick, J. O. "War and Finance in the Anglo-Norman State," *Transactions Royal Historical Society,* 5th Series, IV (1954).

Richardson, H. E. "The Coronation in Mediaeval England," *Traditio,* XVI (1960).

Ridgeway, W. *The Origin and Influence of the Thoroughbred Horse.* Cambridge, 1905.

Round, J. *Feudal England.* London, 1895.

Rudkin, E. H. "Where Did William land?" *Sussex. Arch. Collections,* 1928.

Schram, P. E. *History of the English Coronation.* Oxford, 1937.

Smail, R. C. "The Art of War," in A. L. Poole, ed., *Mediaeval England,* Vol. I, Chapter IV. London, 1958.

Stenton, F. M. *Anglo-Saxon England.* Oxford, 1945.

Turner, G. T. "William the Conqueror's March to London," *English Historical Review,* XXVII (1912).

Waley, D. F. "Combined Operations in Sicily, 1060–78," *Papers of the British School at Rome,* XXII (New Series, IX), 1954.